go ahead.

go ahead.

The invitation awaits. Stay put in the ordinary or go ahead and take a risk on the impossible.

written by

Willow Weston

© 2021 Willow Weston and Collide

All rights reserved. No part of this book may be reproduced or transmitted in any form or by any means whatsoever without express written permission from the author, except in the case of brief quotations embodied in critical articles and reviews. Please refer all pertinent questions to the publisher.

info@wecollide.net

Cover and book design by Lindsey Kiniry

First printing edition 2021
wecollide.net

Table of Contents

1. An Innate, God Given Desire — p. 9
2. Everyday Extraordinaires — p. 21
3. Go Ahead — p. 31
4. Listen in the Storm — p. 51
5. Step out of the Boat — p. 73
6. Limitless — p. 89
7. Power of Fear — p. 107
8. Failing Forward — p. 127
9. Walking Your Friends Towards Healing — p. 139
10. It's Your Turn — p. 151

COLLIDE...
AN INTRODUCTION

> COLLIDE...
> AN INTRODUCTION

The Collide Story

I remember walking into a counseling office over a decade ago because my pain was chasing me down. I had run into Jesus and had even been leading in ministry for years prior to walking in for help, but God was inviting me into a deeper healing than I had yet to receive and perhaps a higher calling than I had yet to understand. I walked in for guidance because my pain was leaking out in ways that scared me. I sat in that counselor's office and stared at her clock as she asked me the all too expected question: "So what brings you in here today?"

I had a run-in with Jesus Christ in that office that had nothing to do with the counselor. God gave me two words: wounded collision. He helped me to see that I was born into pain. I had collided with wounds that were never healed, and they wounded me and now I wounded others. Sometimes it seems like we are all bumping around, colliding and wounding each other. I sat in that room desperate for all of us to have a new kind of collision. My pain was crying out for it.

==When I see Jesus, He collides with people and rather than wounding them, He leaves them more whole.== God's Spirit showed up in that counseling office in a way that pierced the air. God invited me to see those who wounded me from His perspective rather than my own. God called me to enter people's brokenness, instead of running from it. God reminded me that He is, indeed, a God who wipes brokenness all over Himself. I was being invited to collide with Jesus in my brokenness and invite others to come along.

So, I walked out of that appointment holding a spiritual concept, but even more, I knew in my innards that I was being called to do something big with those two words. Soon afterwards a beautiful young college aged girl from church asked if I would mentor her. I wasn't feelin' like the mentoring type right about then. She said she wanted to learn more about Jesus. I invited her to get together and study the Bible and see what happens when Jesus collides with wounded people. She was excited, so excited, that she invited all her friends, because twenty-some college women came knocking on my door.

We spent the next several years looking at Jesus colliding with people in the New Testament and as we did, He collided with us too. When Jesus restored the shriveled man's hand, He too, restored these college girls' shriveled self-esteems. When Jesus said to the woman caught in the act of adultery, "Go and sin no more", He too, said this to the young woman in my living room who had been caught stark naked in shame and Jesus set her free. When Jesus went out of His way to collide with the woman at the well who was

Collide...
An Introduction

going from man to man to man because she was so thirsty, Jesus too, met the college girls in my living room and He gave them something to drink that quenched their parched living. Those twenty girls and I experienced a new kind of collision when we ran into Jesus, one that brought about wholeness.

Most of the girls graduated and moved away from college. There were four girls left and they wanted to keep meeting. I prayed, and God said, "I am not into us 4 and no more Bible studies, it's time they teach the message." I was working as a college minister at the time and this idea came out of nowhere. I had a lot of other things on my plate, not to mention a full-time job, a husband and two kids. God handed us an opportunity to do something to impact lives that was beyond our understanding, but we had to act on His invitation. So, we did an experiment and that experiment led to what is now Collide, this ministry, that invites women of all ages, races, socioeconomic statuses, faith backgrounds, and life places to run into Jesus and as they do, they are forever transformed.

God took a story of pain and brokenness and turned it into this beautiful ministry we call Collide. We shape and craft events, conferences and retreats for thousands of women every year. We now have a counseling program assisting people who desire to walk towards healing in their life. We encourage and support mentoring, where women meet in life changing intergenerational relationships and co-learn from one another. We have a blog that God is using to invite people all around the country to collide with Jesus. We have a podcast which encourages women weekly with engaging content that is reflective of Jesus' love for them. We have a leadership and ministry development program where we are inviting women to tap into God's purpose for their lives. We have a church bridging program partnering with many local churches in the hopes of inviting women to walk a bridge from our events into the local church, so they will keep colliding. We have an amazing staff of gifted passionate, fierce women who are giving their lives away for this mission. And in 2018, we launched our Bible studies which we are creating and sharing in the hopes that more and more people will run into Christ.

I am continually amazed by this Jesus who shows up right smack dab in the midst of our mess and pain and walks us into healing and purpose. Collide has become a place, a community, a movement for so many to run into Jesus just as they are. My hope is that in the same way God met me years ago when I most needed it, He too will meet you right where you find yourself. He is a God who collides... so get ready because He does incredible, big, mighty, miraculous, unimaginable things when you run into Him.

Willow Weston
founder and director of Collide

Collide Values

We value women colliding with Jesus and His teachings.

We value and encourage authenticity (telling our story as it really is).

We value recognizing brokenness, so it can be made whole.

We value the experience and support that comes from an intergenerational community of women of all ages, church backgrounds, life experiences, and faith stages.

We value teaching a theology that runs into the holistic parts of who we are, to encourage a healthy spirituality.

We value pushing towards growth and next steps to go further on one's journey with God.

We value challenging, equipping and inspiring people to serve, lead, minister and use their gifts in order to live into their God-given purpose and change lives.

COLLIDE...
AN INTRODUCTION

Collide invites people of all ages, stages, experiences and faith backgrounds, as imperfect or broken as they may be on their journey, to authentically run into Jesus; as He collides with them, they are forever transformed.

Collide Mission

Who we are and who we aren't

Collide... An Introduction

We are everyday chicks running into Jesus. This Bible study was written, researched and created by ordinary women of all ages, stages and backgrounds, desiring to know God. We have indigestion, PMS, anxiety, and bad hair days. We work jobs, serve on PTA boards, sit on church committees, coach sports and attempt to bless our neighbors. We have different skin colors, different generational experiences, different faith backgrounds and different economic statuses. We like Cheetos and red wine, candles, a good book and a walk on the beach. We get insecure and let fear get in our way sometimes. We battle and wrestle and pray and pray. We have bills to pay, kids to raise, relationships to reconcile and big dreams we'd like to see become reality. We are your neighbors, your friends, your everyday women.

We are not Bible scholars. We have not been to Seminary. We don't have a lot of letters after our name. We don't speak Hebrew or Greek. We are not all that impressive in "religious" circles. If you are looking for that kind of Bible study resource, there are so many great ones, and this might not be the one for you. We merely desire God and are mesmerized by Jesus. We want to learn, grow, study and be challenged and inspired by who God is and who He calls us to be. It is this desire that has led us to run into Jesus and to invite others to come along.

We are still in the midst of our story. We are in chapter 6, not at the end of the book. We have not "arrived." God's not done with us. What we think, feel, or believe might transform, morph, or reconstruct as God continues to collide with us. Who we are now and who we are becoming leaves room for us to be in process, to seek, to ask questions and to be God's kids. We believe God is the best Author and He writes the best story and the story that He is writing in your life and ours is being written as we speak… and so we engage His best story and trust Him for chapter 8, chapter 9 and so on.

We don't have all the answers. We did not set out to write Bible studies because we think we have the Holy Bible nailed down. We do not think we know the answers to all the questions. We don't think we can solve age-old theological debates nor current hot button arguments. We don't think we are tighter with the Big Man upstairs and therefore can tell you all that you need to know. All we know for sure is that God is alive and well. He loves us, and He shows just how much He loves us in Jesus Christ. We know for sure that God desires to collide with us and when we do we are forever transformed. Because we don't have all the answers, we are okay with inviting you, our friends, to come with us as we collide with Jesus

Collide... An Introduction

together. We don't feel the pressure to be know-it-alls, experts or professional "Christians". Neither do we feel we need to provide you with all the answers, easy answers, formulas or a specified spiritual "track" that someone else prescribes. Let's together read, reflect, ruminate and respond. Let's not be afraid to have questions that lack easy answers. Let's not think God isn't big enough to handle our doubt. Let's not limit God to our confusion and misunderstandings. Let's not box Him in either. Let's just collide with Jesus and see what He will do.

We are broken. We have been abused, used, betrayed, judged, manipulated, beat down and lied to. We have skeletons in the closet, a long list of mistakes, shady pasts, paralytic fear and deep-seated bitterness we struggle with. We will not pretend we are someone we aren't, and we won't ask you to either. We are not put together. We are not perfect. We are not immortal. We are not finished, faultless or foolproof. We are not Christian poster children. We are sojourners, inviting you, in your brokenness, to walk alongside us in ours, and together, we will collide with Jesus and by His wounds, we will be made whole.

We aren't afraid to engage our brokenness or yours. We no longer want our past to determine our present. We know that the pain we have experienced can easily walk into all of our collisions and we want more than that for our lives. We want to see our wounds find their Healer. We want to see our pain experience redemption. We want to see our brokenness be used for good. We know there's no other way around pain than to allow Jesus to meet us in it. So, we let Him. We sit in discomfort, we remember, we grieve, we cry, we forgive, we get angry and cry out like the Psalmist. But we don't avoid, ignore or devalue our pain or yours. We believe God meets us where we are. We don't believe you have to get it together before God will run into your life. It is actually in the midst of pain and brokenness that God does His greatest work.

We have big hopes. We believe that this project, to create content that invites people to collide with Jesus, has the potential to change your life and your friends' lives and your neighbors and on and on. We believe this because when people collide with Jesus they are never the same. We see this all the time in our ministry. When people run into who God is, they become who they are made to be. We have big God-sized dreams that when we together, collide with Jesus, we will be changed and then we together can change the world.

Collide... An Introduction

How to use this study

We hand crafted this study for women just like you. It has been designed to be used in the way that works best, personally, for wherever you find yourself. We know that women experience a variety of different roles, seasons, and circumstances. We encourage you to engage this study with your morning cup o' coffee, to pull it out of your handbag while you wait for your kids to be done with soccer practice. Grab it off the shelf when you are struggling to find purpose or invite some friends over and do it together. Jesus meets you along the way, so as you journey, doing whatever it is you do, may you enjoy colliding with Him.

We fashioned this study with freedom and joy in mind. Our hope is that colliding with Jesus brings gratification and not guilt, life and not condemnation, power and not oppression. So please be a friend to yourself and enter into this study with freedom knowing God invites you to come and collide with Him, not so He can critique you or grade you, but so He can love and spend time with you. God doesn't have an expectation of the number of pages you must read or a time-line of how fast you must complete this study. God won't be mad at you if you leave some reflection questions blank or even if you think a question we ask is dumb. It probably is. God merely wants to be with you. Enjoy your time with Him.

We constructed this study with a few simple prompts to invite your engagement.

Read

We will invite you to read a passage of Scripture that unfolds a collision with Jesus and corresponding Scripture that applies. Our desire is that as you see Jesus collide with others, you will also experience this living God collide with you.

Collide... An Introduction

Reflect

Our hope is that you would not just read or "know facts" about the Bible, but instead that you would allow your heart and mind to go to deeper places: to reflect, to think, to mull, to consider. It is in our reflection that God can have some of His greatest conversations with each one of us. And it is in these conversations that transformation, guidance, wisdom and healing take place. We have intentionally written questions that will invite you to purposely reflect so that you can experience just that.

Ruminate

There will be points where we will encourage you to stop and chew, wrestle, learn or meditate on more. This is where ruminating on thoughts, Scripture, and quotes will bless you and invite you further into a collision with Jesus.

Respond

You can't stay the same and go with God. Every time Jesus collides with people they are forever transformed. He often calls us to take action, to pray, to move, to serve, to give, to lay down, to surrender, to not merely be "hearers" of the word but "doers". Our hope is that we will not just "study" God, but that we will become people who respond to our collisions with Jesus in a way that helps us see transformation in our own lives, that then leads to transformation in the lives of those around us.

Leader Guide

When we study God's word together, we hear multiple perspectives which help enhance our experience. If you would like to lead a group of women through this study, we have created a Leader Guide which you will find at the end of this book. Our hope is that this guide will help you lead your group into meaningful conversation as you support and encourage one another.

Let's collide...

An Innate, God Given Desire

1

An Innate, God Given Desire   1

An Innate, God Given Desire   1

I have two teenagers, so there are a lot of new words I'm learning. On occasion I will throw one of these generationally hip phrases into the mix with my kids. Apparently, I use them in all the wrong ways at all the wrong times. And now I almost do it on purpose just to get their eye roll reactions. The kids say "big body benz," so I'll be stretching and say this because my body is bending and my kids will roll their eyes because apparently I'm supposed to use that phrase to describe a hunk with big muscles and carved abs… but not a "hunk" because kids don't use the word "hunk" anymore.

No, that's weird.

I'm supposed to say, "Straight fire," but not be talking about fire. Straight fire is what you say when you see someone catch a touchdown pass with one hand or when you see a ski stunt that could have paralyzed a guy, but instead he nails the landing and a K2 sponsorship. Straight fire is when something is amazing. "Sick" is no longer the description of your status when you have the flu - it's supposed to be a brag that means something is awesome. Apparently calling someone "Jerry" is no longer a name. At my kids' school, it's used as an insult, which really concerns me for all the Jerrys out there in the world.

I should start a confused moms blog. The kids always tell me, "That's so extra. Mom, don't be extra." What they mean is, don't show up to the high school basketball game with snack bags covered in smiley face stickers, passing them out to all the players. When they say someone is extra, they mean someone is excessive, too much, over the top, trying to prove something dramatically. A woman in a sequin shirt and jeans is extra. Note to self. To a teenager, "extra" is coming across like you tried to look good at prom… which I actually tried. I was unsuccessful, but not without effort. Extra is raising your hand in class like you care. Extra is crying in the halls every single time the boy you crush on walks by. Extra is doing a PowerPoint presentation to communicate how you're feeling about a boyfriend. I am being told that extra is a bad thing like sick is a good thing. But if we're honest, I think we all desire to be extra… extraordinary.

I don't know about you, but I'm not shooting for subpar. I'm not hoping to live a life story that can be labeled as inconsequential. I want more than that and I believe you do too. I think one of our greatest fears is that our lives, at their end, with no time left, will be summed up as ordinary and unnoteworthy. The last thing we want to look back and see are chapters described as humdrum, run of the mill, and uninspiring. None of us think of our future and aim to be insignificant. No one is going for mediocre. We don't tune into TED talks that inspire us to live "so so" lives. We don't make vision boards with lofty goals to be decent. We don't set out for college and invest thousands to have nothing to write home about. We don't beg God to answer our prayers to bring about the not-worth-mentioning in our lives. We don't hope people read our biography and yawn. No one is like, "I dream to live a story that no one thinks is worth telling."

An Innate, God Given Desire 1

Reflect

If at the end of your life it could be described as any of the following, how would you feel?

Inconsequential…

Mediocre…

So-So…

Not worth mentioning…

How would you like your life, and how you lived it, to be described?

We want to live extraordinary lives. We want the long and short of the plot to contain exceptional moments along the way. We want the pages to chronicle something remarkable. This desire is why we cry when we watch American Idol, (okay, maybe only I cry) because right before our very eyes is someone who felt muted, dim, unnoticed, and then they are discovered to have within them something out of this world, special, destined. And when they're discovered to be extraordinary, I cry, and that's when those darn teenagers of mine laugh at me. And I say, "That was straight fire."

Our desire to experience the extraordinary is why we set goals and hustle and chase, all in pursuit of something awesome that we cannot now see. This desire for the remarkable is why we pray for miracles. It's why we believe upon God for bigger things than we ourselves can make possible. Our desire to live lives that are far beyond ordinary is why we lean into the work of helping make the world a better place. This desire we have to be a part of something incredible is why we adopt orphans and

An Innate, God Given Desire   1

give money away to help people in need. This desire within us is why we love redemption stories. Brokenness is so real to each of us, that to see redemption and good come from broken places tells us the extraordinary is possible. And if it's possible for her and her and he and them, then maybe it's possible for us.

This desire we have to live extraordinary stories is one we've had since we were little. In elementary school I wrote a book called Willow's Whispers and it was pure cheese. In fact, I found it recently. It has stories about unicorns and plane crashes and a poem about a mouse eating my blouse. For some crazy reason I got picked from my class to travel to a Young Authors Conference and read my book, whose cover was made of tinfoil, to an actual audience. That was one of the first moments I experienced an invitation to be a part of something that offered me the chance to write a story that mattered.

Growing up I loved basketball as much as I loved boys. My best friend's dad was the first black mayor in Washington state. He was also the town's grave digger and the school janitor. Every weekend he would open the school for my friend and me. We would shoot hoops all day. When we were in elementary school the high school girls' basketball team took State year after year. It was such a big deal in our small town, that those of us following in their footsteps were trained up in camps and dreamed to do what they were doing. I remember a special night, maybe in 5th grade, where we each got one of the player's personalized jerseys to wear for an event. They hand picked which varsity players' jersey we each got based on who they thought we had the potential to be like. We came out on stage in our heros' shirts, doing ball drills in front of the entire community. It wasn't just a night to celebrate the phenomenal story of our champs, but there was an invitation for those of us looking up to them, that we too

> If the *extraordinary* is possible for her and her and he and them, then maybe it's *possible* for us.

An Innate, God Given Desire 1

could be a part of something out of the ordinary. That invitation made me shoot more free throws. It made me run lines faster. It made me want to become more than who I'd been.

As a kid, I was a single child with a single parent, so if I didn't entertain myself, ordinary Wednesdays became dreadfully boring. My mother would do accounting at home at night for the cafe business she owned. I would stand there while she punched numbers on a very loud calculator and I would recite Martin Luther King Jr. speeches. My mom would say, "You're such a neat kid." And when I read his words, I dreamed his dream. I could feel a rising up in me that wanted to do something that mattered, like what I was learning was possible. The more I began to hear of extraordinary stories, the more I wanted to live one.

Reflect

When you were a girl, what did you dream to do with your life?

Over time, what happened to those dreams?

Do you still dream dreams for yourself?

An Innate, God Given Desire   1

Each of us has had this desire to live extraordinary lives since we were little girls. In fact, I might even argue we were born with this desire. It is like the umbilical cord that traces us to our Extraordinary Maker. The very fact that we hope to live an extraordinary story is not something to feel ashamed about, not something to hide, not something to downplay or pretend is not within us. This desire is actually how we are supposed to feel. We were given one opportunity to live a story.

I wonder what God, in all His majesty and splendor, in all His sovereignty and power, in all His creative genius and cleverness in making you, might say to you in the moments you succumb to believing your one story might just have to be ordinary and inconsequential?

> This *innate hope*,
> this running after such,
> this *bend we have* to live exceptional stories,
> points to our inherent *desire* for God
> and being in the center of
> God's *best story* for our lives.

There is a famous story in the Bible that we are going to center around in this study. In fact, it's so out of the ordinary that we often don't know what to do with it. In **Matthew 14**, Jesus walks on water to get to His disciples who are in the middle of a storm. The crazy thing about this story is that Peter walks on water too. Peter was in a boat with several other guys, but thousands of years later, guess whose story we are talking about? We aren't talking about anybody else in that boat- just Peter. Why is that? Because Peter took part in the extraordinary and the other guys just watched it.

An Innate, God Given Desire 1

Reflect

Would you describe yourself as someone who watches others take part in extraordinary things or are you taking part in them too?

What is interesting to you about the idea that thousands of years later we are talking about Peter in the story of **Matthew 14** but no one else who was in the boat with him?

How do you resonate with wanting to live a story worth telling?

An extraordinary story worth telling is possible for each one of us. And somewhere along the way, life told those little girls who had big dreams to be a part of something extraordinary, that there's something about us that doesn't make the cut. Life told us that other people are special- they have special talents, special favor, special connection to God, whatever special thing it is we don't feel we have. Life told us to resign to being average because we aren't all that impressive.

An Innate, God Given Desire — 1

Reflect

What have your difficult life experiences told you about your desires to be a part of the extraordinary?

My Difficult Experience	How that experience affected my belief that it's possible to take part in the extraordinary
Unrealized dreams	Told me to give up dreaming
Unanswered Prayer	
Fails	
Storms	

> You can *take part in the extraordinary* or you can watch others.

17

An Innate, God Given Desire 1

I think we stopped dreaming because a few dreams flopped. I think some of us stopped praying because we didn't see results. I think a few of us failed in front of an audience and the embarrassment halted all future risks. I think we hate storms so we stopped going outside. I think our faith moved from asking God to move mountains to thanking God for dinner. I think we once thought we had a fighting chance to do something monumental and now we are just trying to win the war on laundry.

We started to believe that God only lets a few of those He favors in to see His magic tricks. So if you're real talented, if you can sing How Great thou Art like Whitney Houston reincarnated, if you can look good in jeans AND eat cheeseburgers, if you can get people to follow you, if you can recite the Bible, if you can do these kinds of things, then God might invite you in to experience the good stuff.

Reflect

Who or what kind of person do you often believe God favors by giving them extraordinary experiences, giftings, opportunities?

How have you been shamed to no longer believe in big dreams for your life?

An Innate, God Given Desire 1

I think we used to recite Martin Luther King Jr. speeches and the rising up within us got tired and gave up. Culture shamed us for wanting to be a part of something amazing and so we stopped trying. We stuffed those feelings down and agreed with our teenagers, "That's so extra."

Somewhere along the way the little girl in us was torn down, discouraged, mocked, stifled and callused. So now we run through all the reasons God won't show up, all the ways we don't have what it takes to write books and inspire justice like we once dreamed, all the ways we should stay safe, not risk failing and just sit in that boat and watch others take part in the extraordinary because... maybe extraordinary is just not in our reach.

What you have in your hands is a book whose entire goal is to convince you that you, my friend, were made to be part of the extraordinary. And over the course of this study, your fear, your worry, your insecurities, and all the parts of you that stopped dreaming, will be challenged. You will spend time with Jesus and see how He brings about the extraordinary in the most ordinary of people. And your life will begin to be unleashed as you collide with Him. Enjoy the journey and expect God to show up and meet that little girl in you who still has big big dreams.

xoxo,
Willow

An Innate, God Given Desire — **1**

Respond

God, I set aside this time, this space, this walk through this study to collide with you. Will you meet me in my deep desire to live an extraordinary life and will you do something first in me and then through me? God, I ask that you would help me dream again, help me believe again, that you can do amazing things through my life. Meet the little girl in me whose big dreams have been dashed, disappointed and discouraged. Please renew, refresh, reinspire.

Amen.

Everyday Extraordinaires

2

21

Everyday Extraordinaires 2

Everyday Extraordinaires 2

Though we often believe the extraordinary is for others but not for ordinary ol' us, Jesus tells us otherwise. We can see in the story of Peter but also in the story of women all around us that the amazing, incredible and sometimes even unimaginable is possible. Women who feel ordinary are participating in the extraordinary. Every week I get to interview inspiring women for The Collide Podcast who are watching God unfold amazing stories in their lives. (You can find The Collide Podcast on your favorite podcasting platform.) And their stories give me hope for my own. Let me tell you about a few of them...

Barb Demorest faced a storm of breast cancer in her 60's like a gale force wind. Barb found herself in a bathroom at church, not wanting to come out and reveal her mastectomy, when one of her dearest friends walked in with a Victoria's Secret bag and inside was a knit prosthetic breast. Barb put it on, stepped out of that bathroom with dignity and hope and then started Knitted Knockers, which has now given 170,000 other women all over the world, facing the storm of breast cancer, dignity and hope. (Listen to Barb's story in the podcast "From Devastation to Redemption.")

Kelly Welk attended an informational meeting about human trafficking. Kelly felt disturbed by the devastating stories but she also felt ordinary with no big talents or resources to make a difference. Instead of just feeling sad, Kelly asked, "What can I do?" She could host a great party. So she began hosting freedom dinners to raise awareness and funds which led to the birth of Ciderpress Lane, an organization that now helps free women trapped in a life they did not choose. (Listen to Kelly's story in "From Everyday to Incredible Impact.")

Stephanie Broersma faced the tornado of her husband's betrayal. She stepped out of her pain and anger and allowed God to put the pieces of her family back together and then Stephanie wrote a book called *Reclaimed* that is now being used to help other women put the pieces of their families back together. (Listen to Stephanie's story in "Reclaiming Your Marriage After Betrayal and Infidelity.")

Summer Faith was struggling with an unhealthy relationship with food. Instead of staying there, she reached out to Jesus for healing and is now allowing God to use that pain to coach other women through her organization called Healthy, Whole and Free. (Listen to Summer's story in "Getting Healthy - Mind, Body, and Soul.")

Kate Ahl faced the blow of her husband having a breakdown and losing his youth pastor job. They had to go on food stamps with three little ones. Unexpectedly their roles had to reverse out of necessity. Kate had a friend who recognized a gift in her that she couldn't see in herself, so Kate jumped

Everyday Extraordinaires 2

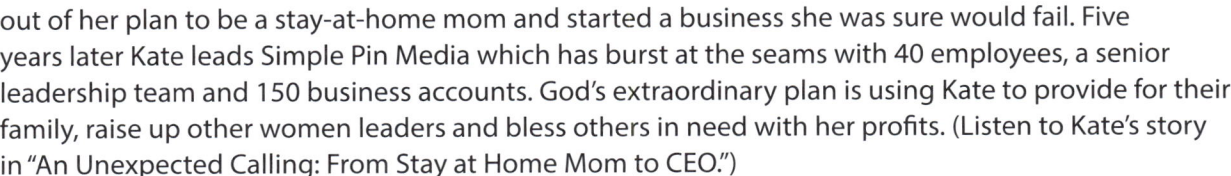

out of her plan to be a stay-at-home mom and started a business she was sure would fail. Five years later Kate leads Simple Pin Media which has burst at the seams with 40 employees, a senior leadership team and 150 business accounts. God's extraordinary plan is using Kate to provide for their family, raise up other women leaders and bless others in need with her profits. (Listen to Kate's story in "An Unexpected Calling: From Stay at Home Mom to CEO.")

Mary Demuth faced the devastation of being sexually abused and experienced the inability of people in the church to know how to help. As God began to heal her, He called her to walk out of her boat of silence. She has written 16 books including *We Too*, calling the church to be part of healing women instead of silencing them. (Listen to Mary's story in "Sexual Abuse, Trauma, and How the Church Can Become a Safe Place.")

Laura Wilkinson experienced the storm of a broken foot that threatened to crush her Olympic diving dreams right before trials. Laura stepped out of disbelief with the odds against her. She trained mentally, literally climbing the diving board on her knees and practiced thousands of dives from start to finish in her head because she couldn't in her body. Her team would cheer for her fake dives as though they were real. Most people would have given up, but Laura banked on Jesus pulling off the impossible and that landed Laura the gold. (Listen to Laura's story in "Purpose Beyond Performance.")

What do you notice all these women seem to have in common?

When you hear stories of other women doing extraordinary things, how do you feel?

Everyday Extraordinaires 2

When hearing other people's stories, do you often feel discouraged about your own life or encouraged by what is possible?

So often when we hear stories of "other" people doing great things, other people who have realized their calling, other people who have outstanding talents, other people who are impacting the world, other people who are successful, we can often feel discouraged. I want to take a few moments with you to help locate what seeing greatness in someone else makes you feel and then allow your feelings to speak. Below is what we are calling an Emotion Spectrum. Certainly there are a jillion emotions you could feel, but we have given you enough that perhaps you can find some you can relate to when you hear stories of other people's extraordinary lives. Go ahead and mark how you feel on the spectrum.

discouraged	**encouraged**
tired	**energized**
apathetic	**excited**
dismayed	**inspired**
overwhelmed	**empowered**
envious	**happy**
defeated	**hopeful**
embarrassed	**proud**
unsettled	**content**
disillusioned	**amazed**
dismissive	**curious**
cynical	**optimistic**
apathetic	**grateful**

Everyday Extraordinaires 2

As you spent time locating your own emotions, what did they tell you?

If you were to sum up your overall emotions when you hear other people's stories, do you often feel discouraged about your own life or encouraged by what is possible?

As you have had time to reflect on the overall emotions you tend to feel when you hear stories of other women doing extraordinary things, what do you notice about yourself?

Friend, I want to pause here. And if this doesn't apply to you, move on forward. But if hearing the amazing feats, the successful accomplishments, the incredible opportunities, the extraordinary stories God has given another woman, if that discourages rather than encourages, we need to deal with what this is bringing up in you. And you are not alone. We have all felt this at one time or another. In fact, in a lot of ways, so many of our culture's voices have invited us to compete with one another, to shame one another, to one up one another, to tear down one another in order to elevate self. But not so with God. God is not so limited, so lacking, so desperate that He can only dole out so much gifting, so much opportunity, so much abundance, so much leadership, so much amazingness.

Everyday Extraordinaires 2

No, God has amazing, incredible, extraordinary things for all of us. One woman's success does not diminish our opportunity to experience success. One woman's giftings does not take away the odds that we have giftings. One woman's chance at overcoming her obstacles does not remove our chance. One woman's miracle did not steal ours.

God shows us other's extraordinary stories, not to discourage but to encourage!!!

We need to retrain our minds. We need to reframe our feelings of envy, of dismay, of being overwhelmed. When we see greatness in another woman, we ought to say this mantra to ourselves, "If God can use her life to do the extraordinary, surely He can use mine too!"

Reflect

What do you think you need to let go of in order to pick up this new mantra?

When you go back through the stories of women doing extraordinary things with this new mindset, how does it change the way you feel about what is possible for your own life?

Everyday Extraordinaires 2

Ruminate

God gives us examples of Him doing the extraordinary in ordinary people to encourage us. Check out these stories and allow them to encourage you. Use the blank spaces to add other examples from the Bible.

Person	What made them ordinary?	How did God do the extraordinary through them?	How does this encourage what is possible in your life?
Bleeding woman **Mark 5:25-36**	She had no status, title or standing that made her anything other than ordinary.	Jesus' power went from His body and healed her, then used her faith to encourage the father of the dying child.	God can heal me and God can use my pain and my faith to help heal others.
Elijah **James 5:17-18**			
Gideon **Judges 6:11-16**			
Boy with bread and fish **John 6:1-15**			
Sarah **Genesis 11:30, 21:1-6**			
Mary **Luke 1:26-38**			
Peter **Acts 12:5-11**			

Everyday Extraordinaires 2

The more I hear extraordinary stories of others, the more I see that an extraordinary story is possible for each of us. Everyday extraordinaires all have

5 traits in common

We will discover throughout this book what those are for our own lives as we walk through Peter's walking on water story.

Everyday Extraordinaires 2

Respond

God, I can see that you do the extraordinary through ordinary people. Help me to believe you can do the amazing through my life. God, help me to reframe my mindset and let go of comparison and envy. Help me to let go of the need to be anyone other than myself, trusting you can do great things through me. God, replace any discouragement with encouragement. I love that you show up in ordinary lives and do the incredible. Show up in mine, Lord.

Amen.

Go Ahead

3

Go Ahead 3

Go Ahead 3

I once took a team of 17 college aged students to Portland, Oregon on a week-long service trip. One day, the mission we worked with loaded up our backpacks with water bottles and granola bars and sent us out with a, "Go ahead, hit the streets!" As I walked around, I started to wonder… What is this granola bar going to do? Will it sustain those who have lost everything? Will it nourish hope into the hopeless? The dealers looked at us like, "Why are you standing on my corner?" The homeless looked at us like, "Don't make me your charity." And I started looking at God like, "Really? You are going to drop me off on the streets with people missing teeth, scratching their flesh off from meth, shooting up heroin like it's an afterschool snack, pimps pimping, and you are going to hand me a granola bar and tell me to go out and do something extraordinary in your name?"

Maybe this is how Jesus' disciples felt too. Maybe this is how they still feel. We are told that God wants to use us in extraordinary ways in the world and that it be possible and we feel like I did that day: unequipped, unsure, unconfident, insecure, scared, doubtful. And yet there I was wandering the streets of P-Town looking for God to do something extraordinary.

²²Immediately Jesus made the disciples get into the boat and go on ahead of him to the other side, while he dismissed the crowd. ²³After he had dismissed them, he went up on a mountainside by himself to pray. Later that night, he was there alone, ²⁴and the boat was already a considerable distance from land, buffeted by the waves because the wind was against it. ²⁵Shortly before dawn Jesus went out to them, walking on the lake. ²⁶When the disciples saw him walking on the lake, they were terrified. "It's a ghost," they said, and cried out in fear.

²⁷But Jesus immediately said to them: "Take courage! It is I. Don't be afraid."

²⁸"Lord, if it's you," Peter replied, "tell me to come to you on the water."

²⁹"Come," he said.

Then Peter got down out of the boat, walked on the water and came toward Jesus. ³⁰But when he saw the wind, he was afraid and, beginning to sink, cried out, "Lord, save me!"

³¹Immediately Jesus reached out his hand and caught him. "You of little faith," he said, "why did you doubt?" ³²And when they climbed into the boat, the wind died down. Then those who were in the boat worshiped him, saying, "Truly you are the Son of God."

³⁴When they had crossed over, they landed at Gennesaret. ³⁵And when the men of that place recognized Jesus, they sent word to all the surrounding country. People brought all their sick to him ³⁶and begged him to let the sick just touch the edge of his cloak, and all who touched it were healed. **Matthew 14:22-36**

Go Ahead 3

This collision between Jesus and Peter invites us to understand that the extraordinary is right outside the place we sit and it's ours for the taking. It's interesting because Jesus had just fed 5,000 hangry people with two loaves of bread and some sardines. (For an in depth study about this, check out our *Yes, You* Bible study). It was an incredible sight to see and the people went mad. They were like the paparazzi on crack. They wanted to force Jesus to be king and Jesus will not be forced into our political demands. We can't buy Him off. We can't impress Him with our earthly titles or sway Him with the promise of followers. Jesus will only be king the way He wants to be king.

The crowd pressed into Jesus so He insisted the disciples get into a boat and "go ahead."[1] You have to wonder, what did Jesus know the disciples would experience by journeying ahead without Him? I would imagine they might have wanted to stay with the crowd and see how all this excitement plays out. But Jesus asks them to go ahead and they do.

Reflect

When God asks you to move away from the crowd, do you listen?

What would have been hard about leaving this scene to hop in a boat and set out from shore?

Jesus gets the crowd to dismiss, which is potentially a miracle in and of itself. Then He famously goes up to a mountainside by Himself to pray. Sometimes the best thing we can do when we are surrounded by people who want to make us something we're not, is to get away and be with our Father.

[1] Henry, M. (1994). Matthew Henry's commentary on the whole Bible: complete and unabridged in one volume (p. 1685). Peabody: Hendrickson.

Go Ahead 3

Reflect

What sticks out to you about the idea that this crowd was trying to force Jesus to be how they wanted Him to be and His first move was to get away and be with God?

How do you feel like sometimes people pressure you to be something you don't feel called to be?

How often do you turn to the Father to be reminded of who He has called you to be when the crowds are pressing in?

> The easiest thing in the world to be is *you*. The most difficult thing to be is *what other people want you to be*. Don't let them put *you* in that position. - *Leo Buscaglia*

Go Ahead 3

When the crowds press into Jesus,

He presses into the Father.

You and I are often pressed by the crowds, by cultural expectations of what a woman, a wife, a mom should be, by social media, by what our body, our house, our social life should look like, by familial expectations, fulfilling long held generational roles, by friends and bosses and neighbors and… and it all gets to be too much. You and I cannot be all things to all people. You and I cannot be what Instagram wants us to be at the same time as what our boss wants us to be at the same time as what our kids hope we will be at the same time as what our eating disorder wants us to be. The pressure of everyone's expectations has the great ability to create anxiety, fear, worry, settling, and giving in. We can lose a clear sense of who God has called us to be. And the best thing we can do when the pressure is starting to be too much is to sit with our Father, the One who made us, the One who calls us, the One who destines our life. He knows exactly who we are called to be. So when we forget, He will remind us.

Reflect

What are some pressures getting to you lately?

Go Ahead 3

How do you see other people's expectations on your life getting in the way of the extraordinary God wants to do in your life?

How can you build time into your life to get away with the Father?

When you do get away with the Father, who do you often hear Him calling you to be?

While Jesus was spending time with the Father, His disciples were travelling in a boat. At one point the boat was 3-4 miles out,[2] surrounded by strong winds and high waves. These guys had been in a storm like this before, but last time Jesus was with them, and this time He wasn't. Last time, Jesus was annoyingly taking a nap while they all peed their pants, terrified. That's when they woke Jesus up and He told the wind and the waves what to do and they obeyed Him. But this time, they are being tormented by a storm and the One who bosses the wind and waves around is nowhere to be seen.

2 Blomberg, C. (1992). Matthew (Vol. 22, p. 234). Nashville: Broadman & Holman Publishers.

Go Ahead 3

Reflect

If Jesus is all-knowing, why would He send His disciples right into the middle of a storm?

Would you conclude that this storm was God's will?

What do you tend to infer from being in the middle of difficult circumstances?

Go Ahead 3

Warren Wiersbe, a theologian, wrote, "The storm came because they were in the will of God and not (like Jonah) out of the will of God. Did Jesus know that the storm was coming? Certainly! Did He deliberately direct them into the storm? Yes! They were safer in the storm in God's will than on land with the crowds out of God's will. We must never judge our security on the basis of circumstances alone." [3]

Wow, what a challenge! Most of us judge our security based on our circumstances. If Jesus sent them ahead, knowing they would face this storm, we can assume, contrary to the cheap faith we have been sold, that being in God's will does not always assure "smooth sailing."

Reflect

Why do we assume being in God's will looks like smooth sailing?

What might God have for these men to learn, gain or witness by allowing them to experience this storm?

Have you learned, gained or witnessed something from experiencing a storm that you can look back upon and be grateful for?

---

[3] Wiersbe, W. W. (1996). The Bible exposition commentary (Vol. 1, p. 51). Wheaton, IL: Victor Books.

Go Ahead 3

The disciples were exhausted from battling the elements all night and around 4 a.m.,[4] they saw what looked like a ghost. They started crying out in fear. The Bible says *"... Jesus went out to them, walking on the lake."* Apparently Jesus didn't have his own raft. These guys come unglued and Jesus says, *"Take courage! It is I. Don't be afraid."* This expression, "It is I," was often used by God in the Old Testament when He revealed Himself.[5] Based on what these guys in the storm heard and saw, they had to wonder if Jesus was actually God in their midst.

God was known to pull off miracles with water. God used Moses to part the Red Sea to set His people free. God wanted to confront an unbelieving nation who had put their faith in Baal, the rain god, so He gave Elijah the ability to declare a drought and a downpour showing them who's actually boss over the rain. God stopped the flow of the Jordan River so that His people would know He was with them. God heard the Israelites complaining of thirst in the desert, wishing to go back to slavery, so God used Moses to call water out of a rock. God saw Jonah running from the call on his life, so He moved His Divine chess pieces. As Jonah got tossed out of a boat, a whale opened its mouth at the right place at the right time to serve as a time out until Jonah could get to a place to say yes to also being at the right place at the right time.

There are so many miracles where God shows He has limitless power over water and Jesus demonstrated the same. Jesus turned water into wine at a wedding two thousand years ago, which some of you still praise Him for. Jesus healed a man born blind with His own spit and mud. Jesus could see through water to know where to catch fish. He demonstrated this crazy ability with Peter one time when he was experiencing some seriously disappointing fishing. Jesus told Peter exactly where to put his nets and the boat became so full of fish it almost sank. Jesus did this again after He beat death like a boss and then showed up to Peter and the guys to say, "Heyo! I'm back." They were out on a boat frustrated because they couldn't catch a darn thing. Jesus directed their poles and they bagged 153 bad boys. And here Jesus was defying gravity and walking on the very waves they feared. I love that

Jesus has the power to trod on the very thing we fear.

4, 5 Morris, L. (1992). The Gospel according to Matthew (p. 382). Grand Rapids, MI; Leicester, England: W.B. Eerdmans; Inter-Varsity Press.

Go Ahead 3

To dive deeper into how God demonstrates His power over water, read: Exodus 14:21-22 & 7:1-7, 1 Kings 18, Joshua 3:14-17 & 4:18, Jonah 1, John 2:7-10 & 9:1-12, & 21:4-6, Luke 5:4-6.

I love what Wiersbe suggests, "Why did Jesus walk on the water? To show His disciples that the very thing they feared (the sea) was only a staircase for Him to come to them…"[6] I love the idea that Jesus will literally walk on the very thing that frightens you to get to you.

What if He could trod on your hypothetical worries and the obstacles to your dreams? What if He could trod on your sense of inadequacy and the big list of things you think you lack? What if He could trod over the brokenness you think threatens your greatness? What if all those things are just His pathway to get you to do something extraordinary?

Jesus will walk to you by way of a storm. That's how much He desires to be with you and me.

---

6 Wiersbe, W. W. (1996). The Bible exposition commentary (Vol. 1, p. 52). Wheaton, IL: Victor Books.

Reflect

What is the very thing, or things, you fear right now in your life?

What if God had the power to trod upon the things you fear?

If God has displayed such limitless power, do you believe the same power is accessible for you or has it somehow expired?

Peter wants to do what Jesus is doing so he boldly yells, "*Lord, if it's you, tell me to come to you on the water.*" I'll tell you what, if you asked me to say a word so you could walk on water, I would say it, just to watch you try. Peter wasn't looking for the ghostlike figure to say the word "come." Peter was looking to hear Jesus' voice.

> Go Ahead 3

Reflect

What is interesting to you about the idea that Peter wanted to hear Jesus' voice rather than just the word "come"?

Have you ever sensed you were hearing God's voice tell you to go on ahead? What did that look like?

When you know God is beckoning you forward, does it give you more confidence to do something you might otherwise question?

Go Ahead 3

You and I want to participate in the extraordinary and so often it's right outside the boat we sit in, just like it was for Peter. And so often the greatest move we can make to experience it is to first believe it is possible. I remember moving from a "how in the world" mentality on the streets of Portland to a posture of faith. I wanted to lead those young college students into an experience where they could truly believe God could use them to bless, impact and change someone's life, because I knew if they could see it to be true, it would change the trajectory of how they chose to live the rest of their lives. But I had to believe it first before I could lead them to believe it. So I looked for God to move. I looked for God to guide. I looked for God to tell us to go right or to go left. I looked for God to show us it be possible that we could experience what could only be Him. I looked for God's "go ahead."

And right there on the Portland street corner watching for God's move, we saw a woman pushing a grocery cart down the middle of a busy road, head on into traffic. And wouldn't you know it, as we stood on a corner unsure where to walk next, this woman's cart came unglued. At first a sweater fell off her cart and then another one and then the whole cart tipped over with everything spilling out. We ran over to help her and she was reluctant to let us pick up her stuff. But she let Matt, one of the students on our team, help. He looked at the wheel that had malfunctioned because a shoestring got caught in it. Standing in what felt like her closet, I asked if we could help put it all back in the tarp. She said no. I asked, "What is your name?"

"April."

April was 40-something, intelligent, kind and strikingly beautiful. I asked her where she was from. She started telling a deeply sad story about coming to Portland with a husband, kids, career and a house. And it's all gone. She didn't even have a picture of her kids to account for any of it. As she started opening up, we started repacking her things. This guy Jimmy, who we knew from feeding him at the mission that whole week, rode by on his bike. We hollered, "Jiimmmmmyyy!" He stopped and we let him in on what was up with April's cart. He didn't have a pocket knife but he had a key to slice the shoestring and a cigarette to burn it off. Collectively, we fixed the cart!

April was headed to relocate under a bridge. It felt like the Spirit had ordained this moment so we asked if we could help her move. After declining a few times, she finally said yes. We hauled a tarp and pushed a grocery cart through the streets of Portland to her new home and she said goodbye. We said, "God bless you. You take care, April," and painfully walked away, disappointed. What good did that really do? What did that teach the students? How was fixing April's cart extraordinary?

Go Ahead 3

A few nights later we were off the beaten path, handing out sandwiches to people and inviting them to a ministry called Night Strike that offers the 15,000 homeless people in metro Portland hot meals, free haircuts and shaves, a place to have their feet washed or get their clothes and sleeping bags replaced. As we were walking away from a sea of people, over to our left we heard a woman's voice yelling toward us. I looked over and it was April! She stood up excitedly in front of her friends to talk to us. We walked over and she was full of joy, much different than what we saw in her a few days before. She said, and I kid you not, "The other day I was going to do something really destructive… I… I was going to stand on the tracks and let a train end all this and you guys inspired me." I couldn't believe it. The extraordinary was possible. It was right outside of my doubt. Then she went on to say, "I want to get baptized and start going to church!"

It is amazing what God can do with water and a granola bar, but even more, with the belief that the extraordinary is possible. And all we have to do is look for God's go ahead. Sometimes it is right outside of a boat. Sometimes it's on a street corner and sometimes it's in your very own house. All I know is that God has extraordinary moments waiting for all of us, but we first must believe they are there.

Go Ahead 3

Reflect

What stands out to you about the Portland story, about this team walking the streets, being sent out waiting and wondering how they were going to pull anything great off?

Do you think this team would have experienced what they did with April had they not been looking for an opportunity for God to use them?

When you think about April, how many "Aprils" do you think are right in front of us but we miss them because we aren't on a "service trip" being challenged to look for them, but instead we are busy with the places we have to go and the things we have to do?

| Go Ahead | 3 |

What strikes you about April's description of how this team impacted her life and the supplies they carried with them to go "do" something impactful?

How do you think you can begin leaning into believing the extraordinary is possible right near where you are, and how can you begin looking for it?

Notice no one else in that boat was looking to hear Jesus' "go ahead." Peter had an audacity about him, but he also had wisdom. He wasn't going to try something without God's vote of confidence. He wasn't going to step out and take a risk without God's invitation. He wasn't going to let his bold ideas be greater than a yes from God. So He asked to hear God's "go ahead." You and I can do the same. We can ask God to speak into our big, audacious, bold hopes and when we hear His yes we can have the courage to step out and do what we are certain feels impossible. And when we do, we begin to see that with Him, it is quite possible because God does the extraordinary with the very ordinary.

Go Ahead 3

Respond

God who holds all power, God who speaks to the wind and the waves and they obey, God who can walk on water, I come before you today and ask that you would speak into my life. I am sitting in a boat and the big, bold, audacious dreams for my life are begging for your invitation, your guidance, your yes. Will you be the One who guides when I step out, when I risk, when I defy my own limits? I trust that you will meet me as you did Peter and when you give me the go ahead, I will move.

Amen.

Start at the Roots

Advice from everyday extraordinaire Kelly Welk

You know, a lot of us say we want to do amazing things, but we often stop at desire, never acting upon it. Kelly Welk attended an informational meeting about sex trafficking and rather than just feel sad about the despair and pain she heard about, she asked God, "What can I do?" That bold question led Kelly Welk to use the giftings and abilities she had to live into the extraordinary calling waiting for her. She is now the founder of Freedom Dinners, which takes the power and community that happens around a table, and utilizes it for the freedom of others. Her work has expanded into Ciderpress Lane, which includes a fair trade shop, online community, and more - all to contribute more to Rescue Freedom in order to liberate people from human trafficking. We can learn from Kelly's story and her advice...

From the beginning there has been a wrestling between light and dark. Through the ages there have been seasons of calm and waves of turmoil and not for one minute has God been removed.

But our humanity loses sight, our hearts begin to believe that He has forgotten us. He's left us to our own failures. And this is exactly where the enemy wants us because our own fear blinds us to God's hand in it all.

It is in the greatest turmoil that we can also glimpse the greatest view of God. When everything is shaken and stirred, disrupted and dismantled - that's when God does His most brilliant work of weaving our hearts to His.

These are the times you can actually feel the foundations your life is built on. It isn't because you hit rock bottom, it's because you built it firm and strong. *'Everyone who hears my words and puts them into practice is like a wise builder who built his house on the rock'* **Matthew 7:24**

Wiggle your toes, stomp your feet and slam yourself into it and feel the foundation so firmly that your heart can gain courage to stare the storm in the face, knowing it cannot shake you. Then shield your eyes from the glare of the turmoil so you can see God's view, muffle the sound of the media so you can hear God's heart and see right in front of you.

Right here in your home, at the very people you live with, look at your neighbor… the one who lives next door or across the street and keep your eyes open for opportunities to love.

This is not a time to wait for grand ideas, it's the time to start at the root of it all - love God and love people in every small way possible.

> Play the game your kids want to play.
>
> Make the dinner your husband, or roommate, loves.
>
> Share zucchini from your garden.
>
> Spend time outside talking to neighbors and being present.
>
> Help mow the yard of your elderly neighbor.
>
> Make an extra loaf of sourdough to share.
>
> Share a cutting of a plant.
>
> Walk your dog when your neighbor walks theirs and talk about life… together.

So where do you start? How can you even make a difference in a world tipped over and on fire? Root yourself on your foundation and reach out to those sinking around you - no one is looking for grand gestures, they are simply hoping to be seen.

Listen in the Storm

Listen in the Storm 4

go ahead.

Listen in the Storm — 4

Read

²⁷*But Jesus immediately said to them: "Take courage! It is I. Don't be afraid."*

²⁸*"Lord, if it's you," Peter replied, "tell me to come to you on the water."*

²⁹*"Come," he said.* **Matthew 14:27-29a**

1. People who live extraordinary stories listen to *Jesus' voice* in their storm.

Peter listened. Barb Demorest listened. Laura Wilkinson listened. Kate Ahl listened. And it was by listening that each knew what to do, when to do, and how to do it. The thunder and lightning, the wind and waves, the fear and the threats, the obstacles and disappointed dreams, none of that drowned out the voice of God to be louder in their lives.

I am so grateful that the first Bible study I ever did was about experiencing God. The truth that God speaks was something I learned right away when I began my relationship with Him in my twenties. When we look for God around every corner, in every closed door and every open one, in breast cancer or an affair, when we listen for Him on mountaintops and in valleys, when we ask Him to speak even in the middle of a storm, He will.

God speaks. Throughout Scripture, God speaks. **Psalm 50:1** says, *"The Mighty One, God, the Lord, speaks and summons the earth from the rising of the sun to where it sets."* Jesus said, in **John 10:27**, *"My sheep listen to my voice; I know them, and they follow me."* God assures, in **Jeremiah 33:3**, *"Call to me and I will answer you, and will tell you great and hidden things that you have not known."* And **Hebrews 1:1-2** suggests God speaks through the life of Jesus. *"Long ago, at many times and in many ways, God spoke to our fathers by the prophets, but in these last days he has spoken to us by his Son, whom he appointed the heir of all things, through whom also he created the world."* Again and again God speaks. And when we come before Him expectant to hear His voice, we start to hear.

Listen in the Storm — 4

Let's talk about 4 ways that God speaks.

1 God speaks through His Word (the Bible).

Ruminate

Read the Scriptures and fill in the blanks.

- *For the word of God is living and active, sharper than any two-edged sword, piercing to the division of soul and of spirit, of joints and of marrow, and discerning the thoughts and intentions of the heart.* **Hebrews 4:12**

    God's Word is _____ and _____.

- *All Scripture is God-breathed and is useful for teaching, rebuking, correcting and training in righteousness, ⁱ⁷so that the servant of God may be thoroughly equipped for every good work.* **2 Timothy 3:16-17**

    God's Word teaches, _____, _____ and trains.

- *Your word is a lamp to my feet and a light to my path.* **Psalm 119:105**

    God's Word _____ our path.

- *For everything that was written in the past was written to teach us, so that through the endurance taught in the Scriptures and the encouragement they provide we might have hope.* **Romans 15:4**

    God's Word provides us _____.

Listen in the Storm 4

- *Therefore everyone who hears these words of mine and puts them into practice is like a wise man who built his house on the rock.* **Matthew 7:24**

    God's Word gives us a _____.

- *So faith comes from hearing, and hearing through the word of Christ.* **Romans 10:17**

    God's Word grows our _____.

Reflect

What is your relationship with God's Word? Do you love it? Despise it? See it as a tool? As a weapon? As a textbook? As a love letter?

If you have issues with God's Word, what are you doing to work through them?

Do you have spaces where you can honestly talk those through?

Do you have access to resources to help you love God's Word again?

What rhythms and habits would be helpful to further invite you to make space to listen to God speak to you through His Word?

For some great *resources* to help you love God's Word again, go to wecollide.net and search for: *6 Places to Go Looking For God and Overcoming the Lies You Believe About Yourself: An Exercise to Replace Lies with Truth and Getting Unstuck: A Reflection to Help Unleash you into the Life you Desire*

| Listen in the Storm | 4 |

2 God speaks through our circumstances.

We can see throughout history, with humanity, God often used a man or woman's hardship, dead end, sickness, need, provision, famine, family line, occupation, God-given gifting, or network, to speak. Spend time below seeing how God used circumstances in people's lives.

Ruminate

Look up the Scriptures and answer the questions that follow.

John 5:1-15

How did God use the circumstances of the man who was waiting on the healing waters, that were not healing him, to lead the man to his true healer?

Luke 5:1-11

How did Jesus use Simon's unsuccess at his job (fishing) to guide him to his future calling?

Genesis 40:13-15, 41:9-13

How did God use Joseph's slavery to one day provide for his rescue?

Listen in the Storm 4

2 Kings 4:1-7

How did God use the woman's lack of resources to help her see the awesome power God could have in her life?

Genesis 3:8-13, 21-24

How did God use the hiding of Adam and Eve to reveal to them the wisdom and teaching that comes from seeing the consequences of thinking we know what's best versus God knowing what's best?

Mark 5: 21-23

How did God use Jesus stopping for the hemorrhaging woman, which could have felt very frustrating to the father of the dying child, to instill in the father the faith to believe the same power that healed the woman could heal his daughter?

John 6:1-15

How did God take 5,000 people's hunger and use it as an opportunity to show them who can provide?

Exodus 9:13-14, 27-28

How did the plagues experienced by the Egyptians guide Pharoah to change his oppressive ways?

Mark 14:30-31, 66-72

How did God use the crowing of the rooster to remind Peter of what Jesus had the foresight to know would happen?

Reflect

How have you seen God use circumstances in your life to speak, guide, direct, teach?

What is interesting about the idea that we often pray and ask God to change our circumstances, and sometimes He does, but sometimes He actually uses our circumstances to change us?

Sometimes it's easier to see how God might be speaking to someone else through their circumstances. Can you think of a few people in your life and how their circumstances might be God redirecting, teaching, prodding, growing, refining, moving, transforming, them?

What do you sense God is saying to you right now using your current circumstance(s)?

Listen in the Storm 4

3 God speaks through people.

Over and over again, the book of wisdom, Proverbs, encourages us to set our life up in a way where we have wise, godly people speaking into our life, our decisions, our dreams, our mistakes. Read the following Scriptures and gain insight as to how wise counsel can better your life.

Ruminate

Read the Scriptures and fill in the blanks.

- *Plans fail for lack of counsel, but with many advisers they succeed.* **Proverbs 15:22**

    With wise counsel, I will _____.

- *Where there is no guidance, a people falls, but in an abundance of counselors there is safety.* **Proverbs 11: 14**

    With wise counsel, I will experience _____.

- *For by wise guidance you can wage your war, and in abundance of counselors there is victory.* **Proverbs 24:6**

    With wise counsel, there is _____.

Listen in the Storm 4

Reflect

Do you have what you would consider wise spiritual counsel in your life?

Is there anything that keeps you from letting those people freely speak into your life?

Is it difficult for you to include other people into the big decisions of your life? If so, why do you think that is?

When you see all that God assures our life will experience if we surround ourselves with wise counsel, why do you think we often fail to do so?

What are you feeling encouraged to do in response to all that wise counsel can offer your life?

Listen in the Storm — 4

4 God speaks through His Spirit.

The Spirit participated in the Genesis of creation.

> *Now the earth was formless and empty, darkness was over the surface of the deep, and the Spirit of God was hovering over the waters.* **Genesis 1:2**

The Spirit breathed life into humanity (Spirit is the same word for breathe).

> *Then the Lord God formed a man from the dust of the ground and breathed into his nostrils the breath of life, and the man became a living being.* **Genesis 2:7**

The Spirit came upon people in great power.

> *The Spirit of the Lord came on him (Othniel), so that he became Israel's judge and went to war. The Lord gave Cushan-Rishathaim king of Aram into the hands of Othniel, who overpowered him.* **Judges 3:10**

> *Then the Spirit of the Lord came on Gideon, and he blew a trumpet, summoning the Abiezrites to follow him.* **Judges 6:34**

> *The Spirit of the Lord came powerfully upon him (Sampson) so that he tore the lion apart with his bare hands as he might have torn a young goat. But he told neither his father nor his mother what he had done.* **Judges 14:6**

> *When he (Saul) and his servant arrived at Gibeah, a procession of prophets met him; the Spirit of God came powerfully upon him, and he joined in their prophesying.* **1 Samuel 10:10**

The Spirit spoke to God's people.

> *The Spirit of the Lord spoke through me (David); his word was on my tongue.* **2 Samuel 23:2**

> *As he spoke, the Spirit came into me (Ezekiel) and raised me to my feet, and I heard him speaking to me.* **Ezekiel 2:2**

The Spirit of God is still creating, still breathing life, still coming upon man and woman in power, still inhabiting the earth and its people.

Listen in the Storm 4

Ruminate

Read the following verses and note what the Spirit does.

- *When the Spirit of truth comes, he will guide you into all the truth, for he will not speak on his own authority, but whatever he hears he will speak, and he will declare to you the things that are to come.* **John 16:13**

    The Spirit speaks _____.

- *But the Helper, the Holy Spirit, whom the Father will send in my name, he will teach you all things and bring to your remembrance all that I have said to you.* **John 14:26**

    The Spirit will help and will _____ you.

- *Likewise the Spirit helps us in our weakness. For we do not know what to pray for as we ought, but the Spirit himself intercedes for us with groanings too deep for words.* **Romans 8:26**

    The Spirit will help you in your _____ and will speak for you when you have no words.

- *The Spirit gives life; the flesh counts for nothing. The words I have spoken to you—they are full of the Spirit and life.* **John 6:63**

    The Spirit speaks _____.

- *But you will receive power when the Holy Spirit comes on you; and you will be my witnesses in Jerusalem, and in all Judea and Samaria, and to the ends of the earth.* **Acts 1:8**

    The Spirit comes in _____.

- *When the Advocate comes, whom I will send to you from the Father—the Spirit of truth who goes out from the Father—he will testify about me.* **John 15:26**

    The Spirit will _____ for you.

Listen in the Storm 4

- *⁸And when he has come, he will convict the world of sin, and of righteousness, and of judgment: ⁹ of sin, because they do not believe in me; ¹⁰ of righteousness, because I go to my father and you see me no more; ¹¹ of judgment, because the ruler of this world is judged.* **John 16:8-11**

    The Spirit _____.

- *And afterward, I will pour out my Spirit on all people. Your sons and daughters will prophesy, your old men will dream dreams, your young men will see visions.* **Joel 2:28**

    The Spirit will pour out prophecies, _____ and _____ on God's people.

God's Spirit is ours to access any hour of the day, anywhere in the world, any mood we are in, any trouble we may find ourselves, any need we may have, any contentment we may feel. God's Spirit is not something we see, like the wind is not something we see. Although when you've been in the Spirit's Presence, you feel like you've experienced something significant. You walk away and think, "That must have been the move and Spirit of God." God's Spirit feels like God's Presence meeting you, nudging you, correcting you, comforting you, counseling you, helping you, encouraging you, reminding you.

God's Spirit always sounds like God. How could God's Spirit be contradictory to God Himself? God's Spirit, is with you. In fact, it was Jesus who challenged our idea that God is to be found in one specific location and He said, *"God is spirit, and his worshipers must worship in the Spirit and in truth."* **John 4:24.** Our desire to connect with God, to find God, to know God, can absolutely be had when we reach for God's Spirit and God's Spirit is everywhere. **Psalm 139** reminds us just how close God's Spirit is to you and me when the Psalmist cries, *"Where can I go from your Spirit? Where can I flee from your presence? If I go up to the heavens, you are there; if I make my bed in the depths, you are there. If I rise on the wings of the dawn, if I settle on the far side of the sea, even there your hand will guide me, your right hand will hold me fast. If I say, 'Surely the darkness will hide me and the light become night around me,' even the darkness will not be dark to you; the night will shine like the day, for darkness is as light to you."* **(V. 7-12)**

| Listen in the Storm | 4 |

Ruminate

Here is how some well known and respected pastors, theologians and teachers describe their experience with the Holy Spirit.[7] Circle the things that stick out to you:

"People from different backgrounds may not have natural affinity, but when the Word of God is treated right and the Holy Spirit is allowed to engage, it can bring together things, people, backgrounds, histories, races, colors, and cultures and hold them together in a way that natural affinity may not be able to do." **Tony Evans**

"Sanctification is the work of the Holy Spirit in us whereby our inner being is progressively changed, freeing us more and more from sinful traits and developing within us over time the virtues of Christlike character." **Jerry Bridges**

"O Holy Spirit, descend plentifully into my heart. Enlighten the dark corners of this neglected dwelling and scatter there Thy cheerful beams." **Saint Augustine**

"Earthly wisdom is doing what comes naturally. Godly wisdom is doing what the Holy Spirit compels us to do." **Charles Stanley**

"The Holy Spirit, thank God, often enables people to forgive even though they are not sure how they did it." **Lewis B. Smedes**

"You may feel overwhelmed by your own poverty and the labors of the day. But if you decide not to wait until you have more strength and more money, and if you pray for the Holy Spirit as you go, you will, when you arrive, know what to do and how to help someone even poorer than you are." **Henry B. Eyring**

"When you're reading the Word of God, you need to let it soak in and let God speak to your heart and let the Holy Spirit work." **Jeremy Camp**

"When the depths are upheld by the Holy Spirit, then the reaction is Christian." **E. Stanley Jones**

[7] brainyquote.com

Reflect

As you read the quotes from other Christians, how do you relate to their experiences with the Spirit?

When you read the verses about the Holy Spirit, what are some action words you notice the Holy Spirit carries out?

Which of these do you need in your life right now?

Have you had experience with God's Spirit and if so, what did it feel like?

Listen in the Storm 4

Teach me to do Your will, for You are my God; Your Spirit is good. Lead me in the land of uprightness. Psalm 143:10

Listen in the Storm — 4

God speaks through His Word, our circumstances, people and His Spirit. One thing to know for sure, God will never contradict His Word, meaning God will never tell you to lie when His Word says, "thou shalt not lie." God will never tell you grace isn't yours for the taking because as you can see throughout the entirety of the Bible, grace wins again and again. God will not agree to your gossip about Suzy and what a terrible sinner she is when God says, "deal with the plank in your eye before the speck in Suzy's." God will never tell you to swim in darkness when He's called you to be the light. God does not speak out of both sides of His mouth, His message will be united through His Word, His counsel, His Spirit and your circumstances. When you are failing to find clarity in what He might be saying, continue praying and seeking His Spirit, and surround yourself by the godly counsel in your life to wrestle over the lack of clarity you feel. Turn to His Word and expect God to speak into your life because He cares about you.

Reflect

How much time do you spend allowing God to speak to you though His Word? (We are pretty proud of you that you are doing it right now in this study).

When you spend time in God's Word, and look at your circumstances and hear from other people and listen for God's Spirit, what do you sense God is trying to say to you right now in your life?

Listen in the Storm 4

The reasons we don't hear God are often the same reasons we don't hear each other:

We aren't familiar with God's voice. John 10:4 says, *"The Shepherd goes on ahead of them, and his sheep follow him because they know his voice."* We have to be in tune with Jesus' tone, inflection, and emphases. We have to spend so much time with Him that we know His character, His every move, His rhythm. We have to soak up His Word in the Bible and memorize it so that it guides like second nature. When you know what the voice of God sounds like, you can decipher it even in the middle of a storm.

We have spiritual selective hearing. We are like spiritual teenagers (at least mine). We can't hear things like, "Do your chores," or "Take out the garbage," or "Walk the dog." But for some crazy reason we can hear, "Here's ten bucks," or "Want some ice cream?" Our hearing listens for what it hopes to hear and everything else we drown out. It's like we have on those noise cancelling headphones my son wears. We wear our pride, we wear our desire to rebel, we wear our bitterness, we wear our hardened hearts, we wear all sorts of God-cancelling headphones and only we can take those off and choose to listen.

It's just too loud. Spotify's on, Alexa's telling jokes, telemarketers are calling, Facebook's dinging, the dog's barking, the calendar's notifying us that we're supposed to be at nine places at once, the Yelp reviews are booing, the alarm clock is sounding, the parents are expecting, the kids are fighting, the boss is demanding, the acquaintances are DMing, the enemies are backstabbing, the culture is pushing, and friends are leaving voicemails. It's no wonder we can't hear anything God is saying.

Our hearts are hardened. In our house I like to say, "The air is thick." No matter what God says He can't win. When I am bitter, mad and resentful, there is nothing someone I love can say that's going to make me want to listen, including God. Maybe you can resonate?

Sometimes we hear God, but we don't like what we hear, so we wait to hear something else. Sometimes we don't hear because we are doing all the talking. Sometimes it's because we're too busy to listen. There are all sorts of reasons we don't hear God's voice, but I'll tell you what, when we desire to hear someone we can even hear silence. I learned this from my kids. When they were little I wanted to hear their voices in the grocery store, at a park, or at a concert in a crowd. I wanted to hear them when they woke in the morning and at night when they were sick. I was so used to listening for them that I could even hear their silence. God speaks but hearing Him requires the desire to start listening.

Listen in the Storm — 4

Reflect

Which of the ways on the previous page might be reasons you don't hear God's voice?

What were some of the things that could have gotten in the way of Peter hearing the voice of God in the storm?

What do you feel led to do to be a better listener so that you can hear God speak into your life?

Peter knew Jesus' voice. In fact, when Jesus and Peter first collided, Peter was with his brother in a boat fishing and Jesus said, *"Come, follow me."* Peter left everything to follow Jesus. And here, much later, Peter still wanted to imitate Jesus. Peter wanted to be in Jesus' orbit because Peter knew that everything ordinary that Jesus touched, He made extraordinary. And Peter wanted that for his life. If we want to be women who participate in the extraordinary, the supernatural, the miraculous, the impossible, the awesome, the amazing, then we need to be women who listen for the voice of God.

Listen in the Storm — 4

Reflect

How fascinating is it to you that Peter was so in touch with Jesus' voice that he knew if he heard it, he would be willing to be the only one in a boat to take a risk to believe the extraordinary was possible?

How important would all the experiences Peter had of listening to and getting to know Jesus' voice be in assuring Peter in that moment on the water that he was indeed hearing the voice of God?

How assured are you that you know if you are hearing the voice of God?

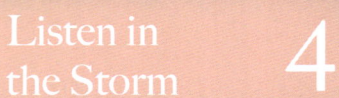

Listen in the Storm — 4

Respond

Oh God who speaks, speak to me. I want to know your voice. I want to know your character so much that I can read your moves. I want to know your heart so much that I can guess what you might say. I want to know your words so much that they guide me when my path feels faint. Thank you for caring about me so much that you promise your Spirit is with me, meeting me, comforting me, directing me, counseling me, helping me and speaking to me. I am here, listening. Help me to follow your voice even onto the waters.

Amen.

Do the Thing

Advice from everyday extraordinaire
Rebecca Dotson George

Rebecca is doing extraordinary work in our world and her work was birthed unexpectedly in the center of her mother's cancer journey. So often we think our extraordinary will come in ways that feel extraordinarily good. But sometimes the big, amazing, extraordinary things God has for us come out of the storm. Rebecca started 818 Ministries, which sews and packages handmade hats with letters of encouragement, delivering them to hospitals all over the U.S. It was in this cancer storm and God meeting her in it, that as she stepped out, He has now grown her work into speaking, writing and hosting the "Do The Thing Movement" Podcast. She did the "thing" and now she wants you to. Check out what she has to say...

We never mean to miss it. We desire that God use us as an instrument to point others to Himself; however, we sometimes allow the enemy to get in the way by discouraging and distracting us from our mission. As one of my favorite writers Jennie Allen says, "The greatest battle our generation will ever face is the battle between our ears." I truly believe people are more passionate and persistent about doing something that matters than ever before. Our issue will never be a lack of momentum. Often, we're divvying out our momentum toward things that really won't matter in eternity.

When I get to heaven one day and see Jesus face to face for the first time, I don't want Him to say, "Wow! Rebecca, you had a really pretty Instagram handle. You were very well connected in society!" Neither of these things are bad but when my head hits the pillow at night, I want to be able to say, "I did all I could today to be one step closer to hearing, "Well done!" from Jesus." Life is too short. Eternity is too long. I want to love God and love my neighbors well in the time that I have here on earth - don't you?

I love in **Hebrews 12** where it talks about laying aside every weight and sin that clings so closely to us. We are to run our race with endurance, free from distractions and ploys of the enemy like insecurity, fear and doubt. We are to look to Jesus, the founder and perfecter of our faith and stay in the lane that He has authored for our life. It's in that lane that we most beautifully can make His name known. Since He made me, He's also more than capable of sustaining me.

We are to "fan into flame" the gifts and talents God has so graciously given us as it says in **2 Timothy 1**. This looks different for everyone and that's what is so beautiful about the body of Christ. What if we all stepped into our calling with full confidence that God is our sustainer and provider? What if we relied on the Holy Spirit as our counselor and helper, giving us discernment and wisdom beyond measure as we move through life?

What is God prompting you to lay aside so that you can "do the thing" He's called you to do?

Step out of the Boat

5

Step out of the Boat 5

Step out of the Boat — **5**

Read

^{25} Shortly before dawn Jesus went out to them, walking on the lake. ^{26} When the disciples saw him walking on the lake, they were terrified. "It's a ghost," they said, and cried out in fear.

^{27} But Jesus immediately said to them: "Take courage! It is I. Don't be afraid."

^{28} "Lord, if it's you," Peter replied, "tell me to come to you on the water."

^{29} "Come," he said.

Then Peter got down out of the boat, walked on the water and came toward Jesus. **Matthew 14:25-29**

2. People who live extraordinary stories step out of the boat and *keep stepping out.*

Notice, no one else in the boat was jumping at the chance to do what Jesus was doing. Why would Peter want to leave the boat? None of us want to leave our boat. It's in the boat that we feel like we are surrounded by company. Our boats promise safety. Our boats are what we trust to assure our security. Our boats are our float plan.

| Step out of the Boat | 5 |

Reflect

Why would it make sense to you that no one else would be asking to step out and walk on water?

What do you think it was about Peter that made him different from the other guys?

What do you do in life to ensure your safety and security?

Would you say you have a personality that is risk averse or do you like to take risks?

Step out of the Boat 5

What would you say is your current float plan- the plan for your life that offers your spirit a sense of security- that if you have this, you will feel safe?

On what conditions would you leave that float plan?

The Thing I know to be true about Jesus is that He is not afraid to call us to leave everything. He will ask us to hand Him our life, our pain, our dreams. He will challenge us to step out of the crowd. He will call us to let go of what falsely floats us, enslaves us, identifies us or owns us. He will challenge us to step away from things we think save us so that He can save us. Jesus will call us to let go of our pride and pick up a cross. He'll also call us to step on the stormy waters if it means that the extraordinary we were made for is on the other side. And though that may scare the heck out of us - what's scarier, stepping out into the extraordinary or living a life that at its very end can be summed up as safe, predictable, and unnoteworthy? Leaving our safety and security sounds frightening but what if you knew it promised participating in the extraordinary when you took that step?

Step out of the Boat 5

circle this OR that

Take this **QUIZ**

safe	risky
predictable	unpredictable
routined	scattered
cautious	adventurous
conformist	nonconformist
controlling	accommodating
questioning	accepting
analytical	instinctual
afraid	trusting

Would you most likely be found with a calculator or a journal?

Do you buy toothpaste because it's the brand you've always used or because it's on sale?

Would you be more likely to want to go with your friend on a 4-day river rafting trip or to see the sequel to the movie you both loved?

Do you like to have all your stops mapped out for a road trip or would you be described more as a "fly by the seat of your pants" kind of a gal?

Do you see disruptions to your routine as gifts or annoyances?

When you walk into a party, do you feel energized by the idea of meeting all new people or do you most enjoy sitting down with someone you know and talking deeply?

Step out of the Boat   **5**

Based on the answers to your quiz, how would you rate yourself on a scale of 1 to 10? Mark where you feel you fall on the number lines below.

Likelihood to take risks

1 . . . 5 . . . 10

Willingness to be uncomfortable

1 . . . 5 . . . 10

Tendency to say yes to the unknown

1 . . . 5 . . . 10

What has this exercise told you about yourself as you think about God asking you to take steps that feel risky?

In the very beginning of this story Jesus said to the guys in the boat, *"Take courage."* Jesus seems to be suggesting that bravery is a choice. You don't wake up with courage. You have to choose it. We often take up fear, worry, hypotheticals, what ifs, and fake stories. We often write the doom story right in the middle of the storm. This breast cancer storm is going to kill me. This dream is going to die. I am going to be crushed by the waves of humiliation if I change directions. The wind of heartbreak is too strong for me to stay strong. What if a sea monster of judgement comes and eats me for a snack? What if my boat, that I need to take me where I want to go, splits in half and I have to float on a piece of it like a scene right out of the Titanic? What ifs are never helpful when we need to be brave. Author John Acuff says, "Bravery is a choice not a feeling."[8]

8 https://acuff.me/2013/10/the-ugly/

Step out of the Boat 5

If you feel brave you might not be facing something that requires it.

brave
[brāv]

adjective

ready to face and endure danger or pain; showing courage.

No one ever feels like facing danger and pain yet bravery moves us because we become convinced that there's got to be something more extraordinary worth experiencing on the other side of the boat than there is in the boat.

How long have you been waiting until you "feel" brave enough to step out of the boat?

What do you think about the idea that you might never feel like stepping out of the boat?

Step out of the Boat — 5

When John Acuff says, "Bravery is a choice not a feeling," how have you been making it a feeling?

What do you feel you need to choose bravery for right now in your life?

I love the Donald Miller quote from his book *A Million Miles in a Thousand Years*. "If you watched a movie about a guy who wanted a Volvo and worked for years to get it, you wouldn't cry at the end when he drove off the lot, testing the windshield wipers. You wouldn't tell your friends you saw a beautiful movie or go home and put a record on to think about the story you'd seen. The truth is, you wouldn't remember that movie a week later, except you'd feel robbed and want your money back. Nobody cries at the end of a movie about a guy who wants a Volvo. But we spend years actually living those stories, and expect our lives to be meaningful. The truth is, if what we choose to do with our lives won't make a story meaningful, it won't make a life meaningful either."

> *If what we choose to do with our lives won't make a story meaningful, it won't make a life meaningful either.* - Donald Miller

Step out of the Boat 5

Peter wanted a meaningful story more than a safe one. He seemed to grasp that the best place to be is with Jesus.

Reflect

How does Miller's statement impact you? "If what we choose to do with our lives won't make a story meaningful, it won't make a life meaningful either."

If Peter wanted a meaningful story more than a safe one, what would that require?

What is interesting about the idea that the safest place to be is with Jesus, even though Peter was in a boat and Jesus was standing in a stormy sea?

What do you think about the idea that you might have to step out, not because you feel brave, but because you want what's on the other side of the leap?

Step out of the Boat   5

Most of the women I admire, the ones who are living extraordinary stories, they jumped. They jumped not because they are particularly better at jumping than you and me. They jumped because they were sure that on the other side of that fear, that leap of faith, that unknown, that risk, that sacrifice, on the other side of those things, was something beautiful, amazing, worthy, whole, extraordinary. The women I know who are everyday extraordinaires acted on their faith, trusting that what God had for them on the other side of the leap was worth risking falling and failure.

I think about one brave woman I know, named Mary, who was abused as a child and decided to write her story and make that giant leap to share it in the hopes of helping other people who were abused and had kept it quiet in the church. Now Mary's great bravery and vulnerability is inviting other women to leap to Jesus for healing and help. When God gave her the "go ahead," sure it was scary. But she can now look back and see why she'd make that scary jump over again. Mary could be sitting in the boat right now, but instead she is doing extraordinary things in people's lives with Jesus.

When I think about extra amazing women, I think about a preacher chick I have admired for years who went through the terrible experience of her husband's affair and betrayal. Lori sailed the grueling, messy ride of having to forgive and heal and trust again, and do it all in the public eye. As she sat in that boat, she experienced God meet her in the storm. He called her to rise up out of the pain, the lies that pain told her and walk through the pain to the other side. Every day she took ordinary steps that felt like huge leaps of faith. At first taking a shower felt like a leap. In every step, Jesus met her and walked her from this ugly awful loss right into redemption, love and trust again. He even wrote her a new and unexpected love story. Lori has been brave, and then brave again, to allow Jesus to use her story to help others in theirs. To watch her step out and rise up, has been absolutely extraordinary.

When I think about extraordinary women who step out of boats I also think about Rose. She attended one of our Collide conferences and then signed up for mentoring. She met her mentor but was in a tough place, struggling with loneliness, addiction, and pain and looking to be loved in all the wrong places. When meeting with her Collide mentor, she was challenged to jump into counseling. As scary as that sounded, she did. I have watched Rose jump from this place of great pain to great healing and now she is serving on our Collide volunteer ministry team, helping other women make the leap towards God. Sometimes "taking up courage" looks like making the leap toward help and healing and when we do, God can write our best chapters.

I also think about my friend Michel who was hiding her gift of writing, afraid to let anyone read what she had to say. And I think about our lunch date where she was tearing up about how impassioned she felt to use her voice and yet she was holding herself back. She knew she needed to make the leap and everything in her wanted to stay in the boat and everything in her wanted to jump. I watched her jump. She was brave. She came out of her closet. She shared her gift with the world and when she did, that was the moment I witnessed in her the extraordinary.

Step out of the Boat — 5

We all sit in boats. We are all afraid. We all have a million reasons why not to leap. But we all have something extraordinary waiting for us on the other side. Let us not wait until we feel brave, but instead let us choose bravery like Peter did. Jesus responds to Peter with a big fat 'go ahead' insinuating it be possible to do the impossible. Everybody else stayed in the boat. But not Peter. Nope, Peter in utter trust lifted one foot and set it upon the waves and began to walk on water. It was so "extra." Peter did something extraordinary and I think that always gets missed. We always jump right away to the part where he sank... But let's stop for half a second and take in the fact that

Peter walked on water.

Reflect

What does Peter walking on water, and not just Jesus walking on water, imply?

If Peter can defy gravity, odds and limitations, might it be possible that you and I can as well?

When you read some of the stories of women who took up courage and stepped out of the boat, how are you feeling inspired?

Step out of the Boat   5

How do you order your life in such a way that odds, limits, order, and possibilities tell you what to do rather than God?

What do you see Peter believing in order to take part in such an extraordinary moment?

When you think about the extraordinary you hope to participate in, what odds or limits seem against you?

How can you live in a way that shows your belief that Jesus has the power to defy those?

If we want to experience extraordinary lives, we need to be willing to step out of our comfort zones, our safety blankets, and our security plans, and risk. We need to step out and keep stepping out. If extraordinary, impossible, unthinkable things await our life on the other side of the boat we sit in, the only way we can get there is by stepping out of what we know and walking toward Jesus because in His presence, all limits, all odds, all obstacles, all storms hold little power in comparison to Him.

Step out of the Boat — 5

Respond

Lord, I want to be a woman who steps out toward you and what you have for me. And I want to be brave to keep stepping out. God will you help me believe there are no limits to what you can do. You are mightier than I am, you are wiser than I am, you are bigger than I am. In you resides all power, all knowledge, all ability, all sovereignty. I believe you can do the amazing in me and around me. Help me not to hold my own life back by the limitations with which I view you and myself. Lord, please give me faith where I lack it. I want to be a woman who steps out in great faith walking toward you, trusting you can do the impossible. God I ask, is there a boat I need to step out of right now in my life? I listen for your voice and I need the courage your presence instills. **Amen.**

Jump Afraid

Advice from everyday extraordinaire
Kristen Mattila

Kristen Mattila jumped from what she was doing to what she was meant to do. She wrestled, struggled, fought and prayed because the idea of jumping from the corporate business world into the nonprofit sector was scary. It meant great sacrifice. It meant less pay. It meant leaving behind all she knew and forging ahead into what was unfamiliar. Kristen heard Jesus' voice call her and she finally made the jump. She is now doing extraordinary work on staff at Collide, helping women collide with Jesus in ways that are leaving them forever changed. When Kristen stepped out of the boat… it wasn't easy, but it was worth it. Be blessed by this everyday extraordinaire's advice on jumping…

For a long time, I sensed that God was calling me into something more and I finally reached the point where I knew I had to respond to the passion that was stirring inside my heart. As the pieces began to unfold, I realized that this was going to mean leaving my corporate job to pursue full-time ministry. I didn't understand the depth of faith that would be required of me.

God often calls us to jump afraid. I didn't fully grasp that until I found myself on the edge of the boat ready to take a step of faith. I was being asked to actually move toward the extraordinary life God had prepared for me, but it was in the middle of a storm that left me with this building tension.

On one hand I held the excitement of what God was calling me to do—I was full of expectation and anticipation at the possibilities. And on the other hand, I felt fear mixed with the reality of what this call would ask of me along the way—the unknown and the sacrifices. I wanted the details to be a bit more ironed out, I wanted to know what the future held and I wanted to step out when I felt safe and comfortable.

I always thought I had to feel brave in order to be brave. But, along the way I read some wise advice, that reminded me that I did not have to feel brave in order to be brave. I realized I could still take a courageous step of faith out of the boat in the middle of the storm and experience something incredible like walking on water even if I was not feeling exceptionally brave in the moment. And that's what I did, I took a deep breath and took a step towards Jesus.

Ever since I took that step, it's been an incredible experience, filled with ups and downs, but I've encountered God providing opportunities I never thought possible, showing up in the simplest moments with provision, inviting me into healing I didn't expect and connecting my life with other women who are boldly living their lives by serving Jesus.

Limitless 6

Limitless 6

Limitless 6

Read

Then Peter got down out of the boat, walked on the water and came toward Jesus. ³⁰But when he saw the wind, he was afraid and, beginning to sink, cried out, "Lord, save me!" **Matthew 14:29b-30**

3 People who live extraordinary stories *trust God's limitless power* when they are being held back by their own limitations.

Limitless 6

Reflect

Before Peter stepped out of that boat he must have run through his list of limitations like we do. What do you think Peter thought were his limitations as he considered stepping out of that boat?

What do you think all the other guys in the boat thought about Peter's idea to walk on water?

What do you see as the things that are holding back your potential to participate in the extraordinary?

We desire to participate in amazing things, but we hyperfocus on all the things we believe limit us from doing so. We think we are limited by our DNA, our personality, our family of origin, our health diagnoses, our speech impediment. We think we are limited by the demons we fight, the emotional baggage we carry and our battle with depression. We think we are limited by a crazy busy schedule, lack of financial resources, and people's expectations. Peter got it- he was limited by gravity.

We're really good at telling ourselves all the ways we suck, all the ways we'll fail, all the ways we don't have what it takes. When we want to be part of something big we make ourselves feel small. My IQ is too low. My butt is too big. My family's too crazy. My relationship with God is too inconsistent. My bank account is too pitiful. My talents are too boring. My hair's too flat. My influence is nonexistent. We use limiting statements like, "I don't deserve more," "I shouldn't try," "I'm not enough," "My dreams will never be in reach," "God won't choose me to participate in something special," "I can't."

Limitless 6

I hear limiting language like this all the time from women. The woman who desires to go back to school says to herself, "I'm too old." **God's power will not be limited by your age.** The woman who wants to adopt says, "I don't have enough money." **God's power will not be limited by your resources.** The woman who desires to be freed from her slavery says, "I'm not strong enough." **God's power will not be limited by your strength.** The woman who wants to break out of the life she calls boring says, "I'm not good at anything." **God's power is not limited by your abilities.** The woman who wants to choose differently than the crowd hears, "You'll look like a fool." **God's power is not limited by what people think of you.** The woman who thinks God is telling her to start something, dismisses it. "You have enough to do." **God's power is not limited by your to-do list.** The woman who wants to impact lives jumps back in her boat after sinking and grabs the oars vowing, "Never risk again." **God's power is not limited by your fear.**

Limiting Language Quiz:
Circle which you often find yourself saying.

I'm too old	I'm not strong enough	I'll be judged
I'm too young	I'm not good at anything	I'm too busy
I always fail	I'll look like a fool	I don't have enough money or resources

What other limiting statements do you make about yourself?

How are your limiting statements helping you?

Limitless 6

limiting
[lim-i-ting]

adjective

Serving to restrict or restrain; restrictive; confining.

How would you say you are restricted, restrained or confined?

As women we spend so much time being so good at limiting ourselves. Maybe we should practice releasing ourselves into the fullness of what God has for our lives. When we do this we start to sound like women who are good friends to ourselves. We would never put a friend down and say, "Yeah, you're right, you don't have what it takes to pull off your big dreams." But we certainly say such things to ourselves. The Bible calls us to love our neighbors as ourselves. Many of us have tried to really work on the loving our neighbor part but forgot the love ourselves part.

Friend, maybe it's time to *start being a friend to yourself.*

Limitless | 6

Reflect

Antonyms for the word "limiting" are words like: encouraging, releasing, liberating, strengthening. What are some statements you can start using on yourself so that you no longer limit you?

Example: I am smart, I forgive myself, I am stronger than I give myself credit for, God made me for a purpose.

Limitless 6

> Move forward toward Jesus, and that's when you get to participate in things that defy all your own limits.

How do you think your limiting perspective plays a role in how you view God and what He's capable of doing?

You can't limit Jesus because you feel limited. You can't predict Jesus' abilities based on yours. You can't suppose Jesus' power based on your weakness. You can't assume that the universal principles that apply to everyone else apply to Jesus. You can't stipulate the conditions and expect Jesus to fit within them. Jesus can do what women cannot. Jesus' power is limitless. If you want to experience the power of God, I encourage you to grab the Collide Bible study, *Personal and Powerful*.

You can list off all the reasons why you can't be a part of extraordinary things but Jesus isn't ordinary. Live by your capabilities and be only what you are capable of! But move forward toward Jesus, and that's when you get to participate in things that defy all your own limits.

Limitless 6

Everything ordinary Jesus touches, He makes extraordinary. Jesus turned a little boy's lunch into a feast for the masses. Jesus walked by a fig tree and showed He had the ability to curse it to wither. Jesus sent demons out of a man into some pigs that ran off a cliff and drowned. Jesus healed a woman who had been bleeding for 12 years and then turned around and raised a 12 year old girl from the dead. Over and over again Jesus displays a limitless power that defies scientific laws and expected norms. Jesus demonstrates power over nature, over evil, over death and promises to share this power with us!

Ruminate

Look up the Scriptures and fill in the blanks.

Jesus has power over nature

Matthew 8:23-27

Jesus showed He has power over _the wind and the waves_.

Matthew 14:15-21

Jesus showed He has power over _____.

Matthew 17:24-27

Jesus showed He has power over _____.

Luke 5:4-6

Jesus showed He has power over _____.

Limitless 6

Reflect

How have you seen Jesus' power reflected in nature?

In **Luke 5: 4-6,** Simon answers Jesus' command to let down the nets by saying, "Because you say so." What extraordinary thing might you be able to experience if you answer Jesus the same way Simon did by believing Jesus has the power?

Ruminate

Jesus has power over evil

Matthew 8:16

Jesus showed He has power over _____.

Matthew 9:32–33

Jesus showed He has power over _____.

Mark 1:39

Jesus showed He has power over _____.

Luke 4:31–35

Jesus showed He has power over _____.

Reflect

Limitless | 6

What circumstances around you seem to be the result of the power of evil?

What do the Scriptures you looked up tell you about the power of evil compared to the power of Jesus?

Ruminate

Jesus has power over healing and death

Mark 8:22-25

Jesus showed He has power to heal _____.

Luke 8:43–48

Jesus showed He has power to heal _____.

John 5:5-9

Jesus showed He has power to heal _____.

Matthew 28:5-7

Jesus showed He has power over _____.

Luke 7:11-15

Jesus showed He has power over _____.

John 11:32-44

Jesus showed He has power over _____.

Luke 8:51-56

Jesus showed He has power over _____.

Limitless 6

Reflect

How are you or someone you love in need of Jesus' healing power today?

Where have you seen Jesus resurrect something that once was dead?

How can you apply the verses about Jesus' power over healing and death to something in your life that needs resurrecting?

Ruminate

Jesus gives power to others

    Matthew 14:28-29

    Jesus shared His power with _____ by empowering him to _____.

    Luke 9:1-2

    Jesus shared His power with _____ by empowering them to _____.

    Luke 10:1-2, 17

    Jesus shared His power with _____ by empowering them to _____.

Limitless 6

Acts 3:1-10

Jesus shared His power with _____ by empowering him to _____.

Acts 19:11–12

Jesus shared His power with _____ by empowering him to _____.

Reflect

Have you ever had an experience when you were empowered to do something you didn't think you had the strength, wisdom or ability to do?

How does it encourage you to know Jesus empowers others?

Limitless **6**

Ruminate

Jesus shares power with YOU

Circle the verses that encourage you most in the place you find yourself today.

I will give you the keys of the kingdom of heaven; whatever you bind on earth will be bound in heaven, and whatever you loose on earth will be loosed in heaven. **Matthew 16:19**

He replied, "If you have faith as small as a mustard seed, you can say to this mulberry tree, 'Be uprooted and planted in the sea,' and it will obey you. **Luke 17:6**

And if the Spirit of him who raised Jesus from the dead is living in you, he who raised Christ from the dead will also give life to your mortal bodies because of his Spirit who lives in you. **Romans 8:11**

All these are the work of one and the same Spirit, and he distributes them to each one, just as he determines. **1 Corinthians 12:11**

So again I ask, does God give you his Spirit and work miracles among you by the works of the law, or by your believing what you heard? **Galatians 3:5**

[20] Now to him who is able to do immeasurably more than all we ask or imagine, according to his power that is at work within us, [21] to him be glory in the church and in Christ Jesus throughout all generations, for ever and ever! Amen. **Ephesians 3:20-21**

For it is God who works in you to will and to act in order to fulfill his good purpose.
Phillipians 2:13

For the Spirit God gave us does not make us timid, but gives us power, love and self-discipline.
2 Timothy 1:7

Limitless 6

Peter didn't step out of that boat because he trusted his own capabilities. Peter trusted Jesus' capability. When Peter acted on faith, he walked on water. When Peter saw the wind and acted on fear, he sank.

Fear sinks you every time.

Peter often did a dance with fear and faith just like we do. One page in his story he experienced a miracle and the next he swam in doubt. When Peter was afraid he would be unsuccessful at his job, he was overcome by negativity. When Peter was afraid Jesus would have to die so we could find life, Peter got in God's way. When Peter was afraid of Jesus' arrest, he lopped off a guy's earlobe. When Peter was afraid to be seen as a Christian, he denied having anything to do with Jesus. Peter failed and sank and ran and hid and denied God. He did in a lifetime, all the things I pack in on your average Friday. We begin to see throughout Peter's life that the more he trusted God's ability and not his own, the more the extraordinary showed up in his story. This tells me that when we act on our belief in God's power, that's when our best chapters are written.

Limitless 6

Respond

God of power, I come before you and where I fail to believe in your abilities, give me faith. And where I limit what you can do and what I can do, God, infuse me with a fierce grasp of your limitlessness. God, I have seen what you can do through nature, through humanity, through weakness, through sin… may your power rest on me. May I access your abilities. God, will you overcome my disbelief, my negative perspective, my victim mentality, my "it can't be done" mindset, my insecurities and all the things that hold me back. Will you do the extraordinary in my life despite my limitations? Thank you Jesus that you can.

Amen.

Own Your Worth

Advice from everyday extraordinaire
Jessica Hottle

Jessica Hottle is an author, a podcaster, a fitness coach, and a speaker. She didn't wake up one morning doing all of this meaningful work but instead allowed God to meet her in her places of pain and in the places she was seeking worth for that pain. It was out of God's healing in her life that she stepped out of the boat, discovered more of who Jesus was and what He had for her life and kept stepping out. She is now a successful online entrepreneur and author of two best-selling books, Know Your Worth and A Worthy Wife. She has written a third book called Own Your Worth. She inspires and encourages thousands by sharing her own personal struggles, victories, and journey through life. She truly is an everyday extraordinaire. Check out some of her advice for us...

I hit my breaking point. I didn't know I was at my breaking point until it happened. I was on a red eye flight home from a business conference when I woke up from a deep sleep where my head felt foggy, my body began to radiate warmth, and everything felt like I was looking through lenses that were all scratched up. At that moment I decided to get up, use the restroom, and the next thing I knew I was waking up on the bathroom floor of the airplane. My breaking point led me to months and years of discovering my own denial of stress, over-work, and trauma. Yet, the words, "God is giving you this to teach you a lesson," left me with weak knees, a head bowed in shame, and hands that just spent hours looking for the answer to the lesson He was trying to teach me.

It left me feeling I wasn't good enough when I kept hearing that God wanted me sick to teach me a lesson. My view of the Father was someone who was handing out sick passes to His children so they could become better listeners. Hearing this impacted how I viewed myself. "We are one with Christ in spirit." (Corinthians 6:17). I didn't want to go to the Healer for healing because I thought He wanted me to have it. Believing this lie kept me sick longer. When I began to know of a Father

I had never heard of before, a Father who wanted me well, it began to change every fiber in my being. It changed who I thought I was in Him to who I really was in Him—a woman of worth with the capability of being well.

We limit our worth when we limit God to our capability and understanding.

Owning your worth can be broken down into three parts.

Part 1: Know what's trying to steal your identity. Who and what are you worshipping? What we worship, we become. You can even worship others' opinions and thoughts so much so that you believe them to be true and real.

Part 2: Who do you believe God is? Who is God to you? Who you believe God to be is also how you believe yourself to be. You are made in His image, therefore if your image of Him is being based on lies, then so too will your identity (Genesis 1:27). If we reduce God to our experiences, then we also reduce ourselves. We are image-bearers. This means how I think about Him also affects how I think about me.

Part 3: Identity is knowing who He is. His love. His character. His nature. Knowing Him allows us to know ourselves. You look like your Daddy. We can't keep trying to figure out our identity without ever opening our Bibles AND applying what those powerful pages say.

Your identity is not in a feeling. It's a person. Your identity is about becoming more like Him every day as you renew your soul to His truth.

Remember this: you will know if you are believing a lie when it leads to any kind of destruction. The enemy comes to kill, steal, and destroy. A lie will lead you down this path.

The Truth will always bring about restoration and healing.

I have learned that God doesn't give us sickness to teach us a lesson. The enemy is who comes to kill, steal, and destroy. When I discovered the true nature of Christ, healing began in my body and my soul. I was no longer fighting the Healer for healing. I was merely receiving what His Son already did for me.

Power of Fear

7

Power of Fear 7

Power of Fear 7

Read

²⁸ *"Lord, if it's you," Peter replied, "tell me to come to you on the water."*

²⁹ *"Come," he said.*

Then Peter got down out of the boat, walked on the water and came toward Jesus. ³⁰*But when he saw the wind, he was afraid and, beginning to sink, cried out, "Lord, save me!"*

³¹*Immediately Jesus reached out his hand and caught him. "You of little faith," he said, "why did you doubt?"* **Matthew 14:28-31**

4 People who live extraordinary stories rise back up and choose not to let fear win.

Peter could have easily let fear win the moment he stepped out and saw the power the wind had to topple him. It's so easy to let fear win because fear is relentless, pushy, and found around every corner. You know what fear is really great at?

Here are 10 things:

1 **Fear is really great at lying to you.** Fear likes to tell you, "You don't have what it takes. You're not strong enough, put together enough, educated enough, funny enough, smart enough, secure enough, loved enough, magnetic enough." Fear's favorite hobby is to sit around and lie to you. Fear is the biggest lie bag there ever was, and you know what, some of us are believing its every word, missing out on the life we're made for.

Power of Fear 7

2. **Fear is really great at convincing you that you have to be like "her."** Fear has you comparing yourself to chicks you think are cooler than you and your assessment has got you paralyzed because you think you have to be like someone you're not. Fear has you caught up in gift envy. Fear's got you convinced that you'll never do anything really tremendous with your life because you'll never be as pretty, as well liked, or as talented as Jenny. Well guess what? If you were supposed to be like Jenny you'd be her, but you're not her, you're you, so stop allowing fear to say you are supposed to be anyone other than who you are.

3. **Fear is awesome at handing you your own rap sheet of lame things you've done in the past to keep you from doing great things in the future.** You haven't been tight with God. In fact you've made some pretty lame choices. Plus you always quit. You have no self control. Your motives are selfish and you're not very consistent. You always fail to back your intentions up with action. Look at your past. Those are the kinds of things fear likes to say.

4. **Fear is amazing at convincing you that not using what you have is better than losing what you have.** Fear will be loud and clear that not trying for success is better than risking failure. You might think like the man in The Parable of the Talents, from **Matthew 25**, who was so afraid of losing his master's money that instead of taking any risks, he buried what he had been entrusted with and hid it away to try and keep it safe. There's no chance of loss by saving what you have, but guess what? There is also no chance of gain.

5. **Fear is super great at keeping you smaller than you should be.** You'll find yourself holding tightly to what you have. You wanna be a singer but you only sing in the shower. You wanna write books, but you're running from sharing your work with actual readers. You wanna go back to school but you're assuming you will always do what you've always done. You want to fight for racial reconciliation and you know you have something to say but you keep silencing your own voice. You want more for your life and its capacity, but you'll always feel small if you keep hiding, hoarding and holding back your capabilities out of fear.

6. **Fear messes with God's math.** Fear suggests we will lose what we have if we spend it. Fear says 1 put to work equals 0 but Jesus says 1 put to work equals 2. 2 put to work equals 4. 4 put to work equals 8. When God does our math, things grow exponentially. Talents, impact, resources, life change, dollar bills, faith. But not if fear's doing our math. If fear's doing our math, we hold onto 1 so we don't lose it and it becomes 0. God's math is different. The way He calculates is this: if we don't use it, we lose it. It was Jesus who said in **Matthew 10:39**, *"Whoever finds their life will lose it, and whoever loses their life for my sake will find it."* So often we live holding back out of fear and yet we have a God who suggests we spend our life to gain it.

Power of Fear — 7

7 **Fear is the expert at getting you to play it safe.** Some of us are fraidy cats. I know I am. We're holding on so tight to what we have. We don't move. We stay right there in that boat. But that's just the thing, God doesn't want us to hand Him back what He gave us. God wants to see that we did something with our life. We are so afraid to lose our reputation, our security, our retirement funds, our social life, our house, our figure, our spending money, our weekends, our identity, our leisure, our opportunities, our status, our position and our freedom… but Jesus assures us that it's in losing what we have, in giving it away, spending it and leveraging it- that we and the world around us gain so much more. Don't be like the guy in the boat who lets fear tell him to play it safe. Be like the guy who stepped out because it was he whose story we are still talking about.

8 **Fear tells you not to trust God.** Fear tells you that God is unfair and He will tell you to "go ahead" for His own amusement. Fear tells you God will watch you sink and laugh so you learn a lesson. Fear tells you God will let you fail because you are a fool to think you could do what He does in the first place. We might want to consider changing our view of God because it is clear in so many people's collisions with God in history that their view of God will absolutely determine the story their life tells. And the same is true for you and me. When we see God as damning, we don't ask for big things. When we see God as always wanting to teach us lessons, we don't see room to become teachers. When we see God as liking to mock our boldness, we dim down our bold desires, dreams and ideas and exchange them for settling. When we see God as untrustworthy, we don't step out of our boat because we aren't convinced He'll catch our fall. Your fearful view of God will write a fearful story. In the same way, your faithful view of God will write a faith filled story.

9 **Fear is amazing at getting you to dig holes and bury things not meant to be put into hiding.** Some of you are hiding your talent, your personality, your wealth, your abilities, even your dreams. You have dug a metaphorical hole and are burying the very things you have been given to use. When you hide it, let it atrophy, put it on a shelf, let it expire, deem it useless, hold onto it for yourself, cover it up, you my friend, are burying the very things God gave you to participate in the extraordinary. It's time to get out the shovel and start digging out what we've buried.

10 **What fear is best at is holding you back!** When we are held back, we limit our potential. We worry about failing. We worry about succeeding. We conserve because we don't think we'll have enough for ourselves if we give it away to others. We don't do what we know we ought to because we might fall flat on our faces with a watching crowd. We give up on dreams and exchange them for mediocrities. We box ourselves out of greatness because we ruled ourselves out of its reach. We let other people's opinions of us boss our lives around. We give an old outcome permission to inform all the rest, assuming we can never accomplish what we hope to. Fear loves to keep us believing settling is just fine, this right here, right now, is all we will ever be or ever do.

Power of Fear — 7

fear has a grip on our lives, holding us back in so many ways. Go back and take a look at the 10 things fear is good at and circle the ways fear has been getting the best of you.

Have you heard the story of the man who was passing by some elephants and was stopped by what he saw? He noticed that these giant beasts who weigh between 6,000-13,000 pounds were tied down in captivity, held back by a small, tiny white rope attached to one leg. "How could this be?" he inquired. "Surely an elephant could snap that small rope and break free into the life it desires at the slight force of its giant leg." So the trainer explained that from a very young age, when elephants are much smaller they used the same size chain to tie them up and constrain them. They are trained and conditioned to believe that they cannot break away. So when they grow up they believe, though it's not true, that the tiny white rope that now replaces the chain, can still hold them back. They will never break free to live the life they were made for, so why try?

You know, I think we are a lot like elephants. And I think Jesus knows that. I think God shows up to collide with us because He wants us to break free. We can run. We can do what we dream to do. We can even handle doing what we don't dream to do but know we are called to. We are stronger than we think. We are braver than we know. We aren't made to walk in circles. We aren't made to think we're helpless with no escape. We weren't given life to assume this is all there is. We weren't made to settle for insecurities, anxiety, baggage, dysfunction, addiction, self centeredness and slavery. We weren't given what we've been given to be held back by fear. Jesus knows that we make tiny ropes stronger than we ought. He knows we get stuck thinking we aren't as capable as we actually are. He knows that we have this huge, amazing, vast life waiting for us but we get stuck, bound by lies in big ways and small.

We need to do battle with fear right now. We need to dig it up and uncover it. Fear is the rope that holds you back- and here is what I'm learning- it has no actual power except for the power you are giving it! And it's when you name it, it starts losing its power. (If fear is something you struggle with, we spend lots of time dealing with it in the Collide Bible study called *The Birds and the Lilies*.)

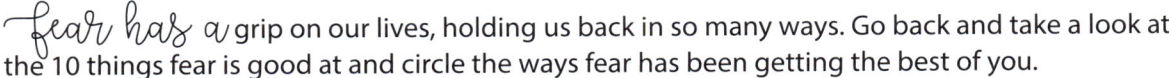

Power of Fear — 7

How do you resonate with the elephant?

What is it that's got a tight hold on you, so much that it's keeping you from living the life you were made for?

How do you see Jesus showing up to collide with people in your own life to break them free from the things that hold them back?

What do you love about that?

Breaking free from fear's grip on our lives starts with us recognizing how much power we're giving the tiny ropes that hold us back. We have got to be women who believe that the power of God is greater than the power of the rope. Do you believe in God's power? Do you believe He is big? Do you believe He is mighty? Do you believe He can break strongholds? Do you believe He can do something new in your life? The elephant will break free when it has the audacity to question everything it believes, everything it's been taught, everything it's been made to think it needs for security and instead believes it has more power than the flipping rope.

Power of Fear 7

Jeremiah 10:6 speaks to the power of just God's name. *No one is like you Lord; you are great, and your name is mighty in power.* **1 Samuel 10:6** says: *the Spirit of the Lord will come powerfully upon you…and you will be changed into a different person.* **1 John 4:4** promises: *Greater is He that is in you, than he that is in the world.* We either stay held back, or we believe we have a God who can bust us free into the full life we were made to live.

The elephant breaks free when the elephant breaks free. Ha! Sounds obvious? You want something fancier, deeper, more thought provoking - that's just it- literally the elephant has to move. The key to breaking free is breaking free. Breaking free looks like you moving your leg that's been tied up way too long by self preservation and safety, worry and anxiety, lies and wrong views of yourself and your God. Breaking free looks like movement. It looks like digging up what you've buried and coming out of hiding. It looks like writing again. It looks like trying to fend off your negative thoughts with painting again. It looks like showing up to work every day, being 100% sure God is going to use you to change lives no matter what it is you get paid for. It looks like singing in front of an audience instead of just in the shower. It looks like applying for that job. It looks like giving yourself the permission slip God already gave you to do something big. It looks like sacrifice and crazily giving away something to bless the socks off someone else even if it means you go without. It looks like facing your greatest fears. It looks like no longer listening to the voices that tell you you're meant for less. It looks like saying, "I will no longer live in captivity." It also looks like saying, "I will no longer live for myself"- because that's just another form of captivity. It's putting out the darn book. It's giving away part of your inheritance. It's waking up every day and believing God gave you your life for purpose. It's deciding to not let anything that holds power over you hold power over you anymore because your God is bigger, your God is stronger and your God is more powerful than anything tying you down and holding you back. And then it's acting on it. The only thing that will break you free, little elephant, is the belief that God can do what you have been made to believe you can't.

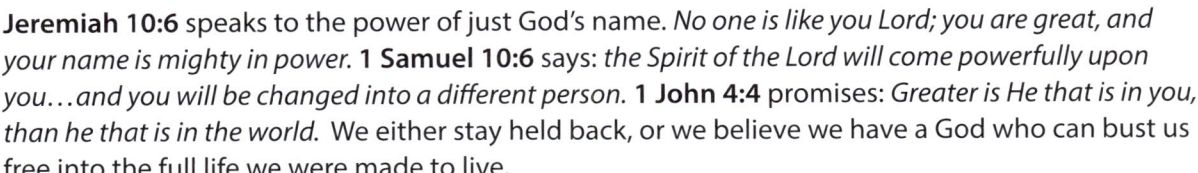

Let's break free, friends, from the *fear* that holds us back!

Power of Fear — 7

Reflect

Are you giving a "rope" in your life too much power? If so, how?

What can you do to live into the belief that God has more power than the "rope"?

What bothers you or encourages you about the idea that in order for the elephant to break free, the elephant had to break free... a.k.a. move?

What is holding you captive in fear that you want Jesus to break you free from?

When fear got the best of Peter, he started to sink and cried out, "Lord save me!" And Jesus reached out His hand and caught him. Jesus saved Peter, which Jesus is in the business of doing. That's why we call Him the Savior.

Power of Fear — 7

Ruminate

God's hand often comes to our rescue. Read the following Scriptures and circle what God's hand does.

Your right hand, Lord, was majestic in power. Your right hand, Lord, shattered the enemy. **Exodus 15:6**

But it was because the Lord loved you and kept the oath he swore to your ancestors that he brought you out with a mighty hand and redeemed you from the land of slavery, from the power of Pharaoh king of Egypt. **Deuteronomy 7:8**

Now I know that the Lord saves His anointed; He will answer him from His holy heaven, with the saving strength of His right hand. **Psalm 20:6**

My soul clings to You; Your right hand upholds me. **Psalm 63:8**

Stretch forth Your hand from on high; rescue me and deliver me out of great waters, out of the hand of aliens. **Psalm 144:7**

So do not fear, for I am with you; do not be dismayed, for I am your God. I will strengthen you and help you; I will uphold you with my righteous right hand. **Isaiah 41:10**

Some of you might need to cry out for some saving right now in your life. God's hand will swoop you up, grab hold of yours and carry you to a place where He can sit with you, teach you, protect you, and love you. All you need do is call on His name. Peter called out, *"Lord save me."* You and I have access to God's saving. We can call out for Him to save our loved ones that are self harming. We can call on God to save our financial woes. We can call on Him to save our alcoholic family members. We can call on Him to save our reputation from someone else's destruction. We can call on Him to save our sinking self esteem. God is a Savior, with a Hand that reaches into all places. I encourage you, friend, to make a habit of calling on your Rescuer in the big things and the small.

Once Jesus rescued Peter, He said, *"You of little faith, why did you doubt?"* Jesus wanted Peter to learn from sinking. Sinking can be life's gift to illustrate faith's power. Sometimes we need to sink so we can recognize the power of faith and the power of fear. One finds us crying out for rescue and the other finds us doing what we never thought possible.

Reflect

What stands out to you about the idea that when Peter had faith, he defied the odds and participated in the extraordinary, but when he had fear he sank?

How have you seen sinking used as a gift in your own life or someone else's?

Is there some sinking in your own life happening right now and what might God use it to produce in you?

Do you think Peter would have recognized the power of faith, had he not experienced sinking?

As Peter learns from sinking, more of his moments, paragraphs, and pages find him choosing faith over fear. By faith, Peter ended up receiving forgiveness for his betrayal, saying yes to God's calling on his life, healing a man who couldn't walk, and raising a dead girl back to life.

> Power of Fear 7
>
> Extraordinary stories aren't always *extraordinary*... sometimes they have *chapters where we sink.*

Power of Fear — 7

As you look at this timeline of Simon Peter's journey with Jesus, what do you notice? Use the space to the right to make notes.

Simon responds with a yes to Jesus saying, "Come, follow me."

    Matthew 4:18-20

    Mark 1:16-17

Simon, in frustration at having no success all night, responds to Jesus with a, "Because you say so" when Jesus instructs him as to where success lies. Simon let down his nets into the deep waters, which was not the common thing to do and he experienced so much success that it almost sank his boat.

    Luke 5:1-11

Jesus sees in Simon who he will become and changes his name to Peter, from the Greek word petros, meaning rock or stone.[9]

    Mark 3:13-19

    Luke 6:12-16

    John 1:35-42

Peter sees Jesus' power when He brings a young girl back to life.

    Matthew 9:18-26

    Mark 5:21-43

    Luke 8:40-56

---

9 Merriam-Webster, I. (2003). Merriam-Webster's collegiate dictionary. (Eleventh ed.). Springfield, MA: Merriam-Webster, Inc.

Power of Fear — 7

Peter is spooked when he sees Jesus walking on the water. Peter listens for Jesus' voice and when Jesus invites Peter to do what He is doing, Peter experiences the extraordinary, walking on water too.

> **Matthew 14:22-34**
> **John 6:16-24**

Jesus proclaims Peter's destiny, saying, "You are Peter, and on this rock I will build my church."

> **Matthew 16:13-20**

Peter tries rebuking Jesus after Jesus predicts He must suffer and die. Jesus in return, rebukes Peter boldly declaring that Peter has in mind the concerns of man, but not of God.

> **Matthew 16:21-23**
> **Mark 8:31-33**

Peter witnesses Jesus' transfiguration on a mountain, "His face shone like the sun and his clothes became as white as the light."

> **Matthew 17:1-13**
> **Mark 9:2-13**
> **Luke 9:28-36**

Jesus has a heart to heart with Peter warning him that he will betray Jesus.

> **Matthew 26:31-35**
> **Mark 14:27-31**
> **Luke 22:31-34**
> **John 13:31-38**

Peter falls asleep while Jesus is praying in the Garden of Gethsemane after Jesus asked him to keep watch.

> **Matthew 26:36-46**
> **Mark 14:32-42**
> **Luke 22:39-46**

notes

Power of Fear — 7

Peter takes out a sword at Jesus' arrest and cuts a man's ears off.

    Matthew 26:47-56

    Mark 14:43-50

    Luke 22:47-53

    John 18:1-13

Peter denies Jesus three times.

    Matthew 26:69-75

    Mark 14:66-72

    Luke 22:54-62

    John 18:15-18, 25-27

Peter is the first to respond to the news that Jesus is alive and runs to the tomb.

    Luke 24:1-12

    John 20:1-10

Peter is the first apostle Jesus appeared to.

    Luke 24:33-34

    1 Corinthians 15:3-5

Peter finds himself in a boat, again, feeling unsuccessful when Jesus shows up.

    John 21:1-13

Peter confesses his love for Jesus three times and Jesus instructs Peter's calling three times.

    John 21:15-17

God uses Peter to heal a lame man who goes from not being able to move to walking!

    Acts 3:1-10

God gives Peter the power to bring a young girl back to life.

    Acts 9:36-43

God rescues Peter by breaking the chains being used to hold him in prison.

Acts 12:1-18

Church tradition states that Peter was crucified upside down at his own request, presumably because he did not consider himself worthy to die in the same manner as Jesus.[10]

John 21:18-19

What stands out to you most about Peter's life?

Simon became Peter over time. How does it strike you that God sees something in you and we can all become something different through our journeys?

Peter often messed up, flubbed up and failed, but he also experienced the extraordinary. What is interesting to you that his story wasn't just one of amazing, powerful, awesome, extraordinary moments, but also had failed chapters?

What do you notice about Peter's character that you admire?

---

9 Bledsoe, S. (2016). Apocryphal Acts. In J. D. Barry, D. Bomar, D. R. Brown, R. Klippenstein, D. Mangum, C. Sinclair Wolcott, … W. Widder (Eds.), The Lexham Bible Dictionary. Bellingham, WA: Lexham Press.

| Power of Fear | 7 |

Peter took a risk when he stepped out of the boat believing he could walk on water toward Jesus. And a life that takes risks is a life that experiences the extraordinary, but it also experiences some sinking. We have to give Peter mad props for taking such a bold move, knowing that sinking was even a possibility. Some of us never even get out of the boat.

You and I want extraordinary lives with no risk, no cost, no discomfort. So much has happened since we were little girls. So now we want a high probability of success before taking a leap because we can't handle the idea of more failure. We want the promise of a zero percent failure rate before jumping enthusiastically like a fool toward Jesus, attempting to do something impossible because we don't want more pain. We want a God who won't ask us to step out on to stormy waters because we don't like to feel unsafe. We want an extraordinary life and a safe God and I am afraid the two do not go hand in hand.

Mark Buchanan, in his book, *Your God is Too Safe: Rediscovering the Wonder of a God You Can't Control*, says, "A safe god asks nothing of us. He never drives us to our knees in hungry, desperate praying and never sets us on our feet in fierce, fixed determination. He never makes us bold to dance. The safe god never whispers in our ears anything but greeting card slogans and certainly never asks that we embarrass ourselves by shouting out from the rooftops. A safe god neither inspires awe, nor worship, nor sacrifice."

What strikes you about Mark Buchanan's challenge of our "safe" God?

How much do you order your life to protect yourself from sinking?

| | Power of Fear | 7 |

Do you do that at the risk of also never experiencing the extraordinary?

What impresses you about Peter in this collision with Jesus?

How would you like to be more like Peter?

If you and I play it safe, that's exactly what our one life will be described as. The eulogy at our funeral will read, "They were such a safe person. They always made sure they had their seat belt on. They never snuck treats into the movie theater. They always protected themselves from looking like they failed. They were so good at steering clear of risk. They didn't waste their time on nonsensical ideas such as miracles and impossibilities and boy did they look comfortable in their Volvo and their boat."

Is this what you hope your one life will be described as?

Power of Fear — 7

Respond

God, thank you that you make the extraordinary possible in my life. Thank you that you lay out the invitation in big and small ways and every day, I get to choose. God, I want to walk toward you and the extraordinary waiting for me. I commit to you in this moment to listen to your voice, to step out of my boat and keep stepping out. Rather than play it safe, God, I trust that you can take my risk, my fails, my steps and my bold hopes and you can show up and do something beyond what I can with all of it.

Amen.

We have a special gift for you, an adorable print of an elephant to remind you to break free from the fear that holds you back. You can download it directly from our website and even listen to a great video message on Breaking Free from the Things that Hold you Back! Find it by searching **Breaking Free** *at wecollide.net.*

Dream Without Fences

Advice from everyday extraordinaire
Carol Beebe

Carol Beebe is one extraordinary woman! She is a successful business owner. She leads her employees, inspiring them to achieve excellence in all they do. She is a certified life coach, guiding clients with clarity and a clear pathway to accomplish their goals, big and small. Carol worked as an educator for over twenty-seven years and brings her background in teaching into coaching her clients. She has also competed in over thirty-five races, including completing two Ironman races. She is not only living an extraordinary life but helping others to do so. Allow her advice on dreams to meet you in the places you feel held back...

Standing at the lake's edge with water lapping over my toes, I anxiously waited for the race gun to go off. Many miles of training had gotten me to this moment. For the past eight months, I had battled through biking and running in all types of weather as well as shivering in early spring lake water to be ready to stand here, shoulder-to-shoulder with twenty-five hundred other anxious souls. I felt confident knowing that I had trained my body physically to accomplish my race goal. Yet, my deeper confidence came from battling the barriers I had in my mind that could have kept me from this dream. Did you know that the biggest barriers you and I face are often the ones inside our head? We create fences (barriers) that can block our progress towards a dream. Our fences are often decorated with words and thoughts (let's call it, dream squashing graffiti) like: fear of rejection, fear of failure, lack of self-confidence, insecurity… Am I smart enough? Am I too young? Am I too old? Words and thoughts that roam around in our heads, keeping our feet firmly stuck at the water's edge.

All of us can have self-imposed fences that keep us from stepping towards our dream. The bigger your dream, the taller the fence! How do you erase the dream squashing graffiti on your fences and replace them with a dream reaching mural? Become aware of your dream squashing graffiti. Spend quiet time reflecting on what is holding you back from stepping into your dream. Is it a fear of something? Insecurity? Past regrets? Ask God to help reveal the words to you. Write your dream squashing words down. Say them out loud. Make visible the words and thoughts that create barriers for you. Awareness of your mind's fences is the first step towards breaking them down.

Then… Dream without Fences.

Now that you aware of your self-imposed fences, dream without fences. Brainstorm around your dream, write it down. Concentrate on the "What" of your dream, you can figure out the "How" later. Some of your dream squashing graffiti may try to sabotage your process, after all they have been roaming around in your head for quite a while! When they do, call them out, "That's just my fear of rejection… Ignore" or, "Look at my insecurity trying to sabotage my dream… Ignore" Replace the sabotage with your dream reaching mural, "I'm so excited!", "I'm confident!", "I've got this!".

Then… Take a small step.

It's time to put your toes in the water! Take one small step towards your dream. Make this first step easy and comfortable. Make one phone call, do a bit of research, share your dream with a person you trust. Do easy steps first to create momentum towards your dream. You will create confidence knowing that you are already walking on the path towards your dream.

Identify your fences, dream without barriers and take a small step or two into the water and… DREAM ON!

Failing Forward

Failing Forward   8

Failing Forward — 8

Read

"²²Immediately Jesus made the disciples get into the boat and go on ahead of him to the other side, while he dismissed the crowd. ²³After he had dismissed them, he went up on a mountainside by himself to pray. Later that night, he was there alone, ²⁴and the boat was already a considerable distance from land, buffeted by the waves because the wind was against it. ²⁵Shortly before dawn Jesus went out to them, walking on the lake. ²⁶When the disciples saw him walking on the lake, they were terrified. "It's a ghost," they said, and cried out in fear.

²⁷But Jesus immediately said to them: "Take courage! It is I. Don't be afraid."

²⁸"Lord, if it's you," Peter replied, "tell me to come to you on the water."

²⁹"Come," he said.

Then Peter got down out of the boat, walked on the water and came toward Jesus. ³⁰But when he saw the wind, he was afraid and, beginning to sink, cried out, "Lord, save me!"

³¹Immediately Jesus reached out his hand and caught him. "You of little faith," he said, "why did you doubt?" ³²And when they climbed into the boat, the wind died down. ³³Then those who were in the boat worshiped him, saying, "Truly you are the Son of God." **Matthew 14:22-33**

5 People who live extraordinary stories risk, knowing that if they fail, they'll fail forward toward Jesus.

Failing Forward — 8

Nothing remarkable can be written about our life without some sort of risk. We are so afraid to fail, but Jesus will catch our fail.

I love my friend Heidi's story because it reminds me that what we often think looks like failure is actually an invitation. Heidi was pursuing a degree in teaching and headed over to New Zealand to do her student teaching. She got all the way over there and the teacher she was working under wouldn't let her teach. She was holding onto this dream of being an art teacher and looking back she even wonders if a college professor who had once pulled her aside and told her she wouldn't be a good teacher, was the reason why she would prove this prof wrong by holding onto this career path even in the face of obstacles. Heidi, being someone who can't just sit around, decided since she couldn't teach she would fill her time by making jewelry with the kids in the cafeteria. She got to experience building beautiful relationships with these kids and outfitting them with the only flare they were allowed to wear to school. The teachers caught on to her beautiful work and her first jewelry shop became the one she set up in the teacher staffroom. When she and her husband returned home from New Zealand it could have been easy to see this "student teaching" pursuit as a fail. But instead of looking for failure, they looked for God.

Heidi's husband nudged her to lean into this jewelry thing and see what could happen. So Heidi hopped on a plane in Washington state and flew to Colorado, rented a car and picked up 20 stores in 2 weeks. Clearly God was opening doors instead of closing them. But then the economy crashed. And she could have looked at this as a fail as well. But she didn't. Heidi got pregnant with her first child and allowed God to remind her that this down time was a gift. When the timing was right, God continued to open doors and for years now, Heidi has watched God unfold her destiny. She is now the Founder and CEO of Heidi Hull Designs Jewelry. She sells her beautiful work in 80 retail stores nationally with opportunities to grow all the time. She is now using her work to bless women in other countries by teaching them how to make jewelry. She is offering them a way out of slavery into freedom by inviting them into her work and giving them a life skill to provide for themselves. If that's not extraordinary, I don't know what is. I think what we can learn from Heidi is that sometimes failing isn't failing. Sometimes it's fumbling toward Jesus and when you get there, realizing it's in the fail and the fumble that you find your destiny.

Peter failed but he failed forward. Here's the difference: Failure mocks you. Failing forward finds you stronger than you were before you stepped out. Failure makes you feel like you still need rescue. Failing forward finds you witnessing your Rescuer. Failure makes you feel alone. Failing forward finds you sinking right into the arms of Jesus. Failure covers you in shame. Failing forward finds you empowered to keep stepping out. Failure tells you never try again. Failing forward finds you in a boat with your God giving a pep talk to get you back out there again.

Failing Forward 8

Reflect

How do you resonate with the idea that Peter failed forward?

How would you describe the difference between seeing things in your life as failing versus failing forward?

How has a failure in your life moved you forward?

I don't know what God is asking you to risk, but knowing Him, He might be asking you to do something really brave. Leaving everything and following Jesus is a risk. Starting something new is a risk. Going in an entirely new direction is a risk. Dreaming again is a risk. Praying for a miracle is a risk. Fighting cancer is a risk. Telling your story is a risk. Stepping foot in church and community is a risk. Getting help is a risk.

Failing Forward 8

Reflect

What is God asking you to risk?

How could it fail?

Why might you be willing to risk despite the fact failing is an option?

Failing Forward 8

> Peter found himself back in the boat with Jesus. This wasn't failure, this was *the making of a great story.*

Reflect

What do you think about the idea that every step of risk, every fail, every moment of sinking can also be the very things that God uses to write your very best story?

How does it encourage you that Jesus got back in the boat with Peter and the disciples after Peter sank?

Failing Forward   8

What did everyone watching in the boat learn from Peter's fail toward Jesus?

What did everyone realize or witness because they experienced one of their friends take a giant leap of faith believing in the possibility of the extraordinary?

Whose life might be impacted by the step God is calling you to take?

| Failing Forward | 8 |

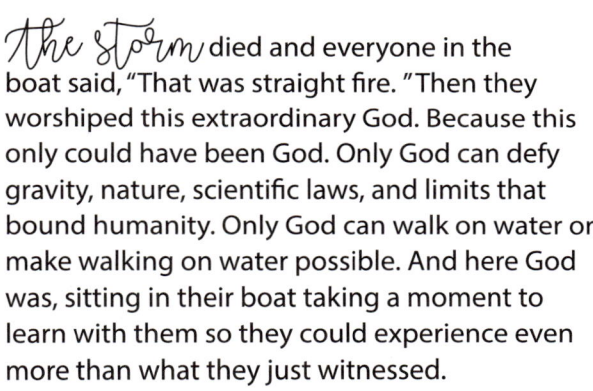

 *The storm* died and everyone in the boat said, "That was straight fire." Then they worshiped this extraordinary God. Because this only could have been God. Only God can defy gravity, nature, scientific laws, and limits that bound humanity. Only God can walk on water or make walking on water possible. And here God was, sitting in their boat taking a moment to learn with them so they could experience even more than what they just witnessed.

You can be sure Jesus would meet Peter in more boats in the chapters ahead and Jesus would call him to keep stepping out of them. And like Peter we get to choose and our choices will determine the story our life will tell. The invitation awaits… Go ahead, stay put in the ordinary or walk toward He who is extraordinary and He'll do in your life what only He can. You choose.

Failing Forward — 8

Respond

God, who made my life, I want to live it as you fully planned, destined, and purposed. When it's fully over, I want my life to be described as _____.
I want to trust you with risks and big steps. Please help me break free from the fear that holds me back. I want to know fully that if I fail, if I sink, if I step out, you will catch me when I fall. God, I trust you as My Savior. When I need rescue I know you will grab me and never let me go. Jesus, I know you came to save and you promise to save all that I ever need saving from. Help me not to be my own Savior and my own protector at the very risk of keeping my life from experiencing all the extraordinary you made it for.

Amen.

Go North

Advice from everyday extraordinaire
Anh Johnson

Ahn Johnson has lived a crazy, beautiful, and meaningful life. She is married and has two young girls. She loves to cook, dress up in inflatable costumes, drink coffee, do late night walks at Target, and enjoy rest with her family. She immigrated to the United States from Vietnam as a child. She knows the obstacles an immigrant faces. She knows the challenges a woman faces. She knows the barriers a female in ministry faces. She is now a bi-vocational church planter that planted a house church called New Legacy. She is an ordained Assemblies of God pastor and is being used to bless the people she has been called to serve. She has an incredible story of listening to the voice of God as He called her and she obeyed even when obeying looked crazy. Listen to this everyday extraordinaire's advice…

There are a handful of times in my life when I recall hearing the audible voice of God. The call to "go north" was one of those times. I remember that day so clearly. I was on a Mother's Day prayer retreat at a beautiful lake. My heart had been wrestling through some things with the Lord. I was trying to make sense of the season. It felt like a holy discontentment. Something had shifted in my heart and it felt like roots were being pulled out. My husband sent me on that prayer retreat to go wrestle things out with the Lord while he cared for our tiny typhoons (our daughters). I heard the Lord tell me to "go north" so I finished my prayer retreat and went home. I wanted to share that word with my husband because I knew that the Lord would not cause di-vision (two visions) in our marriage. Riley, my husband, confirmed the word that the Lord had given me so I resigned from my full time associate pastoral role that night.

By June, 2017 we were living with my in-laws 2 hours north of where we were living. We didn't have a home, I did not have a job, and my husband did not have his job transfer. We had God's word, the prayers and support of our people, and we had the strong desire to show our girls that obeying God is more important than our comforts and plans. There was one major city north of where we lived and where I pastored so I assumed the Lord meant that city because I always assumed that I would be a pastor in an urban area with immense cultural and racial diversity. God had other plans. Now I pastor a home church in a smaller city that is historically known for its Dutch Reformed roots and windmills.

We had the faith to follow God's word, but we spent a lot of time trying to make His "go north" plan fit inside of our plans for where in the north we wanted to live. Some obedience is better than none, right? Wrong. God asks us to obey FULLY, not partially. We rob ourselves of Kingdom promises when we withhold our obedience to God's plan for our lives. I didn't want to move to this town God was calling me to because I couldn't see myself here. How was I going to fit inside of this historically Dutch town as a pastor? I am a tattooed, pierced Asian female pastor from a big city who always dreamed of being a pastor in a diverse urban area. I was so fixated on how I couldn't see myself here that I failed to see what God was doing. I realized that my own ideas, plans, and insecurities were limiting God. When we limit God, we are limiting ourselves in Kingdom work.

I always tell people that I don't share this story of how fast we left our established life and my full time ministry position to go north to no pastoral job, no home and no friendships as a way to toot our own horns. We went quickly because my husband and I both had a united vision and a deep peace about the call. We knew we would find reasons to delay our obedience. We would have justified it because sometimes the call of God doesn't make sense right away. Look at Abraham's call to leave all that he knew to go to a place that God would show him. Look at David's call to lead a nation when his pedigree was leading sheep. Or even Deborah who led a nation into battle and worship in a predominantly male-led culture. God doesn't reveal all the details to the call. He reveals our heart to us by how we respond to the call.

Walking Your Friends Towards Healing

Walking Your Friends Towards Healing — 9

Walking Your Friends Towards Healing   9

Read

³⁴When they had crossed over, they landed at Gennesaret. ³⁵And when the men of that place recognized Jesus, they sent word to all the surrounding country. People brought all their sick to him ³⁶and begged him to let the sick just touch the edge of his cloak, and all who touched it were healed. **Matthew 14:34-36**

Wow, imagine this boat getting to shore. These guys had been through a lot! And here they were. Was the journey over? Just getting started? They had just experienced a frightening storm, witnessed a miracle, watched their friend sink, saw the storm calm, observed Jesus rescue Peter, and then had God in the flesh sit in a boat and teach them. They have been up, what appears to be, all night and here they are on the shores of Herod country.

Reflect

How do you think these guys feel right now?

How do you suppose they are different getting out of this boat than when they first got in it the night before?

No sooner had they docked their boat than people recognized Jesus in their midst. People had heard about Jesus. His reputation preceded Him. It still does. And so often we see, in collisions with Jesus, when people heard He was near they came flocking.

141

Walking Your Friends Towards Healing — 9

Fill in the blank spaces of the table.

Collision	Lengths they took to get to Jesus	Posture in coming to Jesus	What they were hoping for
Luke 5:17-26	They unroofed the roof to get their friend to Jesus	Expectant, humble, persistent	Healing for their friend
Luke 17:11-18			
Mark 5:21-34			
Matthew 8:5-13			
John 4:43-54			
Mark 8:22-25			
Matthew 15:21-28			

Walking Your Friends Towards Healing 9

As you can see, people of all walks of life came running to Jesus when they heard He was in their vicinity. Leaders sought Him out. Desperate people hungered for His help. Those who were told they shouldn't touch God with a ten foot pole, they defied all the social restraints put on them and came anyway. There is just something about Jesus that is so magnetic, so mesmerizing, so life changing, that you cannot help but come and see. Jesus' very presence removes fear from people who would ordinarily stay at a distance from God and others. Jesus' supernatural ability seems to have the power to fight everything in the way of humanity and God. Jesus' healing touch promises something that those who are very far away will travel rough conditions, just to come near. And so they did. Matthew says, *"people brought all their sick to him."*

There are a lot of people who are sick in our lives. We have friends and family walking through the hardship of cancer, heart disease, and diabetes. We have loved ones facing dementia and strokes and the grief is immense. We have friends who feel sick because they live in a deep, dark depression that attempts to keep them in bed every day. We have friends who have mental illness that has wreaked havoc on their lives. We have kids with learning disabilities and we watch them struggle and if we could take it away, we would. Just like that. We have people in our lives who are addicts and their addiction is creating other sicknesses, stealing the beauty right out from underneath their feet.

When you think about the people in your life that you deeply love and care about, who you'd want nothing more than a healing for, who are they? Who would you want to bring to Jesus on the shores of where you live and hope He helps them as soon as you show up?

> Use this box to write the names of people in your life who need healing.

Walking Your Friends Towards Healing 9

Sometimes we need friends who will walk us toward help and healing. What a friend we have, who will recognize the pain we are in and carry us where we need to go. What a friend we have who will come alongside us in our sickness and invite us to the possibility of a cure. How brave is it to walk each other to the One we all need?

Reflect

What are some ways you can walk the people in your life who are sick and hurting to help and healing in Jesus?

Do you think some of the people who brought their sick friends felt nervous to invite them along?

Why do you think sometimes we are so afraid to offer help to people who might need it?

Walking Your Friends Towards Healing — 9

> Carry each other's burdens, and *in this way* you will fulfill the law of Christ. *Galatians 6:2*

Why do you think we sometimes don't ask for help when we need it?

What if our friends who feel sick, want our help, but just like us, don't know how to ask?

The thing that is crazy about this story in **Matthew 14** is that people had such high needs and hopes but also such great faith and expectations in Jesus, that they merely reached out and touched the hem of His robe and they were healed. Jesus was wearing blue and white tassels woven together like what is described in **Deuteronomy 22:12**, *"Make tassels on the four corners of the cloak you wear."*

These people touched just the fringe of His garment and they experienced the extraordinary.[11] Jesus is that powerful. And He honors our reach. Sometimes we just need to reach out and believe Jesus has something for us. And I love that this community came to Him by the dozens believing just that. And they were healed.

---

11 Keener, C. S. (1993). The IVP Bible background commentary: New Testament (Mt 9:20–21). Downers Grove, IL: InterVarsity Pr

Walking Your Friends Towards Healing   9

Jesus honors our reach

I want you to imagine with me for a minute, being here and seeing this sight for yourself. You are standing on the shore of Gennesaret. It has been a long night and you are now different than you were yesterday. You have seen the power of God. You have witnessed Him as a Savior. You have sat in His grace right along with the fish scales at the bottom of a boat. You have watched Him boss the wind and the waves around. You have sat underneath His teaching. You are tired and wonder, isn't He? And here come, over the hill, people in wheelchairs, people whose skin is pasty because they haven't seen the light of day in far too long, people who have skin rashes. You see mothers bringing crying babies and fathers carrying their kids with fevers to Jesus. You see people with sickness like the sicknesses you are watching your friends and family have to endure. And they come to Jesus hoping He will do something.

Reflect

How do you feel right now?

What have the disciples seen, witnessed and experienced in Jesus' character and ability in the last day?

> **Walking Your Friends Towards Healing** 9

If you were one of the disciples in that boat and you had witnessed what they did, how would you feel about Jesus' ability to do something with all the need that stands before Him on this shore?

How does what we have seen God do in the past help our belief when we need faith for the present?

What have you seen God do in your life or others in the past that you can claim to strengthen your faith for this present time?

My guess is that Peter and his buddies had full confidence that Jesus had the ability, the power, the know-how, the grace, the cure, the supernatural might, and the healing touch to meet each person and extend to them all they needed the moment they reached out and touched Him. I don't think these guys were overwhelmed or worried about whether or not Jesus could do something. I think these guys had seen what Jesus could do. I think they got front row seats.

Walking Your Friends Towards Healing 9

They knew Jesus could do what no man can. They knew that Jesus could show up and defy gravity. They knew that Jesus could take the ordinary and do something out of this world, incredibly and extraordinary. My guess is they sat back and at first watched, but then joined in on the weeping, happy tears, gratitude and celebration. For the rest of their lives they would certainly face more storms, they would sink, they would experience sickness in those they loved and even themselves. But they would take with them what they knew to be true about Jesus. And you and I need to do the same. We need to hang our hat on what we have seen God do. We need to claim His character. We need to remind ourselves that the God who fed the 5,000 on one shore is the same God standing in our storm. And the God who rescued us from the storm is the same God our sick loved one stands before even now.

So often when I am struggling, when I don't feel like God is moving, when I don't see a way out, when I'm hurting for someone and begging for mercy, I will do this thing. And I say "thing" because I'm not even sure what to call it. But I will try to invite you into doing this "thing" too. I can be in my car, I can be in the shower, I can be on my knees, bedside, praying. You can do it wherever, whenever. But when I really need God and my faith questions His power, His existence, His ability to show up, I pray like this:

I have seen you do this, God please do this.

God, I have seen you save my son's life, will you save my friend's life?

God, I have seen you provide when I needed it most, can you provide now?

God, I have seen you make a way where there was no way, make a way for them.

God, I have seen you change lives, will you change their life?

God, I have seen you call me and completely do a 180 in my life, will you do a 180 in hers?

Walking Your Friends Towards Healing — 9

Sometimes you and I have to draw back on what we have already seen God do. And sometimes drawing back has to go way far back to what God did with Peter and what God did with Moses, what God did with the woman caught in the act of adultery, and what God did with the Centurion. And sometimes we have to draw back on what God did when we first found Him and what He did when He mended up that childhood pain we never thought could be stitched. Sometimes we have to go back to the time He paid our rent when we had no money in the bank. And sometimes we have to go back to this morning and remind ourselves of the sunrise that keeps rising up in all its hot pink glory. In order to be women of faith who bank on God being able to do the extraordinary in the ordinary, we have got to count on God being who God has always been: able, capable, powerful, magnificent, majestic, mighty, omniscient, sovereign, healing, good, saving.

So, my friend, I invite you to begin doing this "thing" too. We can be women who count on God to be who He already has been. And it will be in these deep draws from the well of faith that we are given the courage to keep reaching out, trusting Jesus has something for us and all who we love.

Walking Your Friends Towards Healing 9

Respond

God I have seen you _____

and now I am asking you to _____

God I have seen you _____

and now I am asking you to _____

God I have seen you _____

and now I am asking you to _____

God I have seen you _____

and now I am asking you to _____

God I have seen you _____

and now I am asking you to _____

Amen.

It's Your Turn

10

It's Your Turn 10

It's Your Turn — 10

We all want to live extraordinary lives. People who live extraordinary stories all have these 5 traits in common. So let's set some goals to increase our everyday extraordinaire traits. Some of us are nailing some of these and lacking in others. Which of the traits below would you like to increase in your life and what are some actual measurable steps you can take to grow in these traits?

1

Everyday extraordinaires listen to Jesus' voice in their storm.

2

Everyday extraordinaires step out of the boat and keep stepping out.

3

Everyday extraordinaires trust God's limitless power when they are being held back by their own limitations.

4

Everyday extraordinaires rise back up and choose not to let fear win.

5

Everyday extraordinaires risk, knowing that if they fail, they'll fail forward toward Jesus.

It's Your Turn 10

Make it happen....

Trait I would like to **grow**　　　3 **action steps** I can take to help me grow this trait

1 _____

2 _____

3 _____

1 _____

2 _____

3 _____

1 _____

2 _____

3 _____

It's Your Turn — 10

There is a purpose, a destiny, a story your life is waiting to write and it's time to lay aside the fear, lay aside the insecurities, lay aside the comparison game, lay aside the doubt and pick up faith. What do you need to set down so you can begin believing an extraordinary story for your life is possible?

Think of all the things you need to lay aside. Write them inside the boat and leave them there.

It's Your Turn 10

Dream journal

We started this entire journey together talking about the dreams we had when we were little girls. I wonder, is it time to re-dream? Is it time to begin believing that your big, hairy, audacious goals might be possible? Is it time to grab hold of the God-sized dreams for your life and begin to lean into the idea that they are yours for the taking? I think it's time. It's time to start to start looking forward with hope and anticipation to what God can do in and through your life. It's time to give yourself permission to wonder what you could pull off with this one great life of yours. On the following pages is space to help you begin dreaming again.

What do you find yourself *dreaming* you could do with your giftings and abilities?

What do people *praise you* for and encourage you to do more of?

DO YOU HAVE A *passion* THAT KEEPS NAGGING AT YOU?

IF YOU COULD TAP INTO THAT, WHAT DO YOU DREAM YOU COULD DO WITH IT?

When you picture yourself doing what you feel made to do, what do you picture?

Want to keep discovering and unfolding the dreams you have for your life? We have some helpful resources for you! Head to wecollide.net/blog and search 'Dreaming for Your Life Again.'

When you dream about making the world a *better place*

how do you envision your part in that?

Is there something you've been hiding out of fear that you dream to bring out and introduce *to the world?*

Do you have a prayer you often find yourself groaning to God, wishing something might become your reality that maybe you feel bashful admitting to others? *What is that dream?*

Is there something you've always longed to participate in that you can give yourself permission to participate in? What would it take to do so?

IF THERE WERE ABSOLUTELY NO BARRIERS IN YOUR WAY, WHAT WOULD YOU DO *right now?*

WHEN YOU DREAM ABOUT WHAT MIGHT BE SAID ABOUT YOUR LIFE, WHAT DO YOU HOPE *sums it up?*

It's Your Turn — 10

Friend, you have beautiful dreams and I cannot wait to see what God does in your story. I am so proud of you for choosing to collide with Jesus, trusting Him to meet you in this study. My greatest hope is that you would begin believing that an extraordinary life is possible for you. That it's right outside every boat you sit in. That it's within your reach. That Jesus' power is yours for the taking. That God will use you in what feels ordinary to you and He will do in your life, beyond what you can imagine. I love that you have gotten brave enough to begin to dream again! Keep dreaming and as you do, listen for His voice because He will speak to you. Step out even if you're afraid. He will honor that risk. Don't limit your abilities, instead lean into your limitless God. Don't let fear win, instead you move, girl! Break free into the life He has for you! See sinking as a gift and always, always, if you're gonna fail, fail forward toward Jesus. I cannot wait to hear the way God takes your dreams, your risks, your bravery, and your faith and writes the very best, most extraordinary stories with them!

xoxo,
Willow

It's Your Turn **10**

Respond

Let's close in prayer:

God, I hand you these goals and these dreams. Do with them what you will. I trust that you have the power and the might to do in my life far beyond what I can now imagine. I leave in my boat all the things I need to set aside all that I need to and I commit to trust you Jesus. I will follow your voice wherever it leads me. I will jump afraid if I am jumping toward you. I will take risks believing in your Presence, I can even defy the odds. Jesus be with me on the journey. Not only do I need you, I want you. Thank you for making everything you touch extraordinary. Touch my life and write a story that in the end can be summed up as beyond ordinary. **Amen**

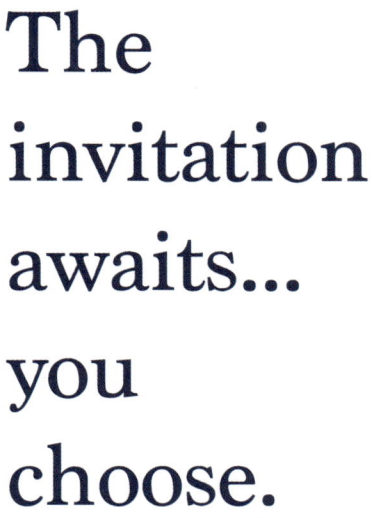

The invitation awaits... you choose.

You *staying* in the boat or you *stepping out* will determine what story your life will tell.

Leader Guide

Leader Guide

We cannot express how much we think leading a group of women centering around a passage of Scripture where Jesus collides, will change lives! Your sacrifice, investment, service and care of these women has the capacity to change their family lives, their friendships, their stress and anxiety, their dreams and their sense of purpose! We cannot wait to hear the ways Jesus collides with you and your gathering of women as you walk them through this study! We have put together a 90-minute experience you can walk women through each time you meet together, covering each part of the study. Please be prayerful, give yourself grace and feel free to cut, edit or add to the experience as you feel so led! If you hate a question we suggest, skip it. If you think of some fun engaging activity that will add to your group's experience, do it! We trust that God is leading you and we merely give you this leader's guide as a tool to use as you see best. May God collide with you as you invite others to collide with Him!

Leader Guide

Section 1
An Innate God Given Desire

Supplies needed:
Collide Bible Study Book
Bible
Blank piece of paper for each woman

Leader (15 minutes)

Welcome!

Invite each woman to introduce herself by answering the following 3 questions:

- *What is your name and why are you excited to be a part of this study group?*
- *Open your phone and pick one picture in the last 10 pictures you took on your phone and tell us what is special, funny or interesting about it.*
- *Who is someone you consider to be extraordinary and why?*

Group (10 minutes)

Read Matthew 14:22-36.
Reflect

- *When you were a girl, what did you dream to do with your life? Over time what happened to those dreams?*
- *Willow stated on p. 15, "The very fact that we hope to live an extraordinary story is not something to feel ashamed about, not something to hide, not something to downplay or pretend is not within us." How have you been made to feel like wanting to live an extraordinary life is too "extra"?*

Partner - optional (10 minutes)

Reflect

- *Split into groups of 2 or 3 and share with each other something you reflected upon in your table on p.17.*

Leader Guide

Group (40 minutes)

Reflect

- *What did you learn about the correlation between some of the experiences in your life and your belief that it is possible to take part in the extraordinary?*
- Discuss answers to the first two reflection questions on p. 16.
- *When you think about that boat full of men, what strikes you about the idea that thousands of years later, we are talking about Peter and not the other guys?*
- *What do you think keeps you often watching other people participate in the extraordinary instead of participating in it yourself?*
- *Willow poses a question in Part 1… try and give it some thought… "I wonder what God, in all His majesty and splendor, in all His sovereignty and power, in all His creative genius and cleverness in making you, might say to you in the moments you succumb to believing your one story might just have to be ordinary and inconsequential?"*

Individual (10 minutes)

Activity

- Give each woman a blank piece of paper.
- *Look at the way you answered the question on p. 18 about how you have been shamed to no longer believe in big dreams for your life. What if a friend wrote the answer you did? What would you say to her? Spend a few minutes writing a note to your "friend" to encourage her.*

Leader (5 minutes)

Respond

- Tell the group what you hope they will gain from the next 10 weeks to help them live into the extraordinary that God has planned for each one of them.
- Pray aloud for the group, the prayer on p. 20 making the pronouns fit a group instead of an individual.

Section 2
Everyday Extraordinaires

Leader Guide

Supplies needed:
Collide Bible Study Book
Bible

Leader (15 minutes)

Welcome!
- Invite everyone to participate in a question web. As the leader, start by asking one woman a fun "would you rather" question. Try and keep with the extraordinary theme. (Ex: Would you rather be a New York Times best selling murder mystery author or be a famous YouTube vlogger? Would you rather be amazing at making cheesecake or amazing at weaving baskets?) After the first woman answers, she asks another woman who has not yet been asked and so on and so forth.

Group (20 minutes)

Reflect
- *We are going to spend some more time this week exploring the concept that it is often easier for us to see that the extraordinary is possible for "other" people but not for us. Was there anything that came up for you this week that made you realize how often you think this?*
- *Which of the examples of everyday extraordinaires inspired you most and why?*
- Discuss the reflection questions on p. 24-25

Partner - optional (10 minutes)

Reflect
- *Split into groups of 2 or 3 and share your experience with the Emotion Spectrum. Use the reflection questions on p. 26 as a guide.*

Leader Guide

Group (35 minutes)

Reflect
- *How do we reframe our minds to begin thinking, "If God can use her life to do the extraordinary, surely He can use mine too!"?*
- *What are some practical things we can do, as women, to encourage one another in our own pursuit of an extraordinary life?*

Ruminate
- *Turn to the table on p. 28 where you looked up ordinary people who God did the extraordinary through. What struck you most from doing this exercise?*
- *What were some of the ways they were "ordinary"?*
- *How was Peter ordinary and how do you see God showing up and doing the extraordinary in His life in* **Matthew 14** *that we read last week?*
- *What did you notice about God as you watched Him in each of their lives?*
- *How did this encourage what is possible for you in your own life?*

Leader (10 minutes)

Respond
- *What is one way you need encouragement today?*
- Pray aloud for the group, incorporating the encouragement women shared they need.

Leader Guide

Section 3
Go Ahead

Supplies needed:
Bible Study Book
Bible

Leader (10 minutes)

Welcome!
- *What are some ways you have started to notice more women living out extraordinary traits?*

Group (40 minutes)

Reflect
- *Have you ever been tasked to do something important and yet you felt unequipped, unsure, unconfident, insecure, scared, doubtful? Tell us about it.*
- *In the same way that Willow didn't think water and a granola bar was going to change lives on the streets of Portland, what do we often think we need to pull off the extraordinary?*

Read Matthew 14:22-36.
Reflect
- Discuss the questions on p. 34.
- *Consider the quote by Leo Buscaglia in the margin on p. 35– "The easiest thing in the world to be is you. The most difficult thing to be is what other people want you to be. Don't let them put you in that position." How do you sometimes feel others trying to make you be something you aren't?*
- Discuss the questions from p. 35.

173

Leader Guide

- *If Jesus is all-knowing, why would He send His disciples right into the middle of a storm?*
- *Would you conclude that this storm was God's will?*
- *What do you tend to infer from being in the middle of difficult circumstances?*
- *Why do we assume that being in God's will looks like smooth sailing?*
- *What might God have for these men to learn, gain or witness by allowing them to experience this storm?*

Partner - optional (15 minutes)

Reflect

- *Break into groups of 2 or 3 and discuss what you have learned, gained or witnessed from experiencing a storm that you can look back upon and be grateful for?*

Group (15 minutes)

Reflect

- *What do you think about the idea that God can trod upon the very things you fear? What would you like Him to trod upon?*
- *What is interesting to you about the idea that Peter wanted to hear Jesus' voice rather than just the word "come"?*
- *What was it that made Peter trust Jesus' go ahead?*
- *What ordinary things did God use on the street corner to do the extraordinary, impacting April, the homeless woman who lost everything?*
- *You and I want to participate in the extraordinary… what do you think about the idea that so often it's right outside the boat we sit in?*

Leader (10 minutes)

Respond

- Ask women to share one thing that consistently seems to hold them back from answering Jesus' "Go Ahead."
- Incorporate the answers the group gave in your closing prayer.

Leader Guide

Section 4
Listen in the Storm

Supplies needed:
Bible Study Book
Bible

Leader (10 minutes)

Welcome!

- *We are about 1/3 of the way through this study and this week we start looking at the 5 traits everyday extraordinaires have in common. What traits have you seen in Peter that you are starting to notice you'd like to emulate on a daily basis?*

Group (10 minutes)

Read Matthew 14:27-29a.

- *People who live extraordinary stories listen to Jesus' voice in the storm.*

Read Matthew 14:27-29a.

- *What strikes you about the idea that Peter was listening for Jesus' voice in the storm?*
- *What could have gotten in the way of Peter listening?*
- *What might have kept the others from listening?*
- *What do you think gets in the way of you listening for God's voice in your own life?*

Leader Guide

Group (60 minutes)

Reflect

- *Of all the things mentioned that keep us from hearing God's voice on p. 67, which do you attribute most to your spiritual hearing problems?*
- *What do you think about the idea that, "the reasons we don't hear God are often the same reasons we don't hear each other"?*
- *Of these 4 ways God often speaks (His Word, our circumstances, people, and His Spirit) which do you most often experience God speaking through?*
- *Which of the 4 ways God speaks feel foreign or challenging to you?*
- *When you think about the things that get in the way of your hearing God and you think of the way He speaks, what do you feel encouraged to do to listen more to grow your relationship with God?*
- *Peter knew Jesus' voice… how did he know it?*
- *Why do you think Peter was the only one who had the audacity to try and do the extraordinary? Would he have had this audacity if he didn't know it was Jesus out there walking on the water?*
- *What if Peter had not known Jesus' voice previous to this moment, this storm?*
- *What do you think about the idea that a lifetime of getting to know Jesus' voice will prepare you for the storm and for the extraordinary chapters in your life?*

Leader (10 minutes)

Respond

- *Since we have been spending a lot of time talking about hearing God's voice, I want us to close by spending some time just listening. I am going to be silent for a few minutes and you can close your eyes, you can leave them open. You can open your hands palms up ready to receive, you can get cozy somewhere. Do what you need to do, but most of all carry yourself with a posture of faith, believing God can speak. And allow Him to meet you right now. In a few minutes I will close in prayer. (Close in prayer.)*

Section 5
Step out of the Boat

Leader Guide

Supplies needed:
Bible Study Book
Bible
Journals or blank pieces of paper

Leader (10 minutes)

Welcome!
- *How have you been more intentional about listening to God's voice this past week?*

Group (15 minutes)

Read Matthew 14:25-29.
- *People who live extraordinary stories listen to Jesus' voice in the storm.*

Reflect
- Discuss the reflection questions on p. 76.
- *How do you feel about the idea that Jesus is not only not afraid to ask you to step out your boat, but that He most likely will ask that kind of bold, faith-filled, audacious move on your part?*
- *Leaving our safety and security sounds frightening, but what if you knew it promised participating in the extraordinary when you took that step?*

Leader Guide

Individual (15 minutes)
Activity
- *Spend some time going back over the quiz you took on risk. You already answered the question about what this exercise told you about yourself, but let's spend some time thinking about some other things. I will read some questions and then give you a few minutes to write your answers in the margin or a journal or paper or whatever you want to use.*
  - *What is the difference between taking a risk and being cautious of a dangerous situation?*
  - *What do you most often do when weighing the pros and cons of a risk and how does that usually work for you?*
  - *What is one risky thing you sense God is asking you to do?*
  - *What is one step you can take this week to move toward taking that risk?*

Group (40 minutes)
Reflect
- *Does anyone want to be brave and share the one risky thing they sense God is asking them to do?*
- Discuss the reflection questions on p. 80-81.
- Read the Donald Miller quote on p. 81 and discuss the reflection questions that follow.
- Take some time to stop for a minute and really discuss the amazing miracle that Peter walked on water. Use the reflection questions on p. 84-85 as a guide.

Activity
- Have women use a piece of paper to write in large letters one limit they are facing. Then have women hold up their papers one by one and invite the group to respond with a statement of encouragement back to her.

Leader (10 minutes)
Respond
- Close in prayer, specifically calling out some of the odds/limits women wrote down and the fact that God has the power to defy them.

Leader Guide

Section 6
Limitless

Supplies needed:
Bible Study Book
Bible

Leader (10 minutes)

Welcome!

- *Last week we talked a lot about risk and how God has the power to defy the limits we see in the way of taking those risks. Did anyone have the opportunity to do something that felt risky this past week?*

Group (35 minutes)

Read Matthew 14:29b-30.

- *People who live extraordinary stories trust God's limitless power when they are being held back by their own limitations.*

Reflect

- Discuss the reflection questions on p. 92.
- *This week as you thought about limiting statements, what did you notice about the limiting language people around you use?*
- *When you hear other women making limiting statements about themselves, what do you want to say to them?*
- *What self-limiting language do you often use?*
- *What do all of our limiting statements do for us?*
- *Can you call out some of the statements you came up with from the exercise on p. 95 to help you stop limiting yourself?*
- *How convicting is this statement: "You can't limit Jesus because you feel limited"?*

Leader Guide

Partner - optional (10 minutes)

Ruminate
- *Find a partner and discuss the questions about Jesus' power from p. 97-102.*

Group (25 minutes)

Reflect
- *What do you think about the idea that Jesus shares His power with you?*
- *Which of the verses about that had the most significance for you and why?*
- *What strikes you about the idea that Peter did not step out of the boat because he trusted his own capabilities?*
- *What happened in Peter's life when he acted on faith in Jesus' power?*
- *What happened when he didn't?*
- *What principle can you draw from this to apply to your own life?*

Leader (10 minutes)

Respond
- *What is one way you are limiting God in your life that you want prayer for?*
- Close in prayer by incorporating some of the answers to the question above into your prayer.

Section 7
Power of Fear

Leader Guide

Supplies needed:
Bible Study Book
Bible

Leader (10 minutes)

Welcome!

- *Last week we talked about God's limitless power. Did you find yourself noticing your own limiting language? Did you stop and remember anything we learned about God's power?*

Group (5 minutes)

Read Matthew 14:28-31.

- *People who live extraordinary stories rise back up and choose not to let fear win.*

Partner - optional (30 minutes)

Reflect

- *Break into groups of 2 or 3 and discuss the 10 things fear is great at.*
  - *How have you seen fear lie to you or someone you love?*
  - *How does fear have you comparing yourself to others?*
  - *When has fear reminded you of your past failures?*
  - *How does fear convince you to keep what you have to yourself?*
  - *What in your life has become smaller than it should be?*
  - *What have you lost because you didn't use it?*
  - *When have you played it safe?*
  - *What misconceptions about God has fear created?*
  - *How can you begin to dig up what you've buried?*

Leader Guide

Group (35 minutes)

Read aloud the story of the elephant from p. 112.

Reflect

- Discuss the reflection questions about the elephant story from p. 113.
- *Do you believe that the power of God is greater than the ropes that hold you stuck in place?*
- Discuss the reflection questions on p. 115.

Ruminate

- Invite women to read each of the Scriptures on p. 116.
- *Which of these Scriptures has the most impact on you and why?*

Ruminate

- Discuss the reflection questions on p. 117.
- *How do you see people living life in a way that shows they want a zero percent chance of failure?*
- Read aloud the Mark Buchanan quote on p. 122 and discuss the questions that follow.

Leader (10 minutes)

Respond

- *What do you feel like God has been saying to you this week as you studied this?*
- Close, praying for the women after they share.

Leader Guide

Section 8
Failing Forward

Supplies needed:
Bible Study Book
Bible

Leader (10 minutes)

Welcome!
- *Did anyone do anything last week to break free from a rope that's been holding them back?*

Group (25 minutes)

Read Matthew 14:22-33.
- *People who live extraordinary stories risk, knowing that if they fail, they'll fail toward Jesus.*

Reflect
- *What struck you about Heidi's story?*
- *Have you had a similar experience in your life where what looked like a failure found you right where you were supposed to be?*
- *Based on your experience, Heidi's story, and Peter's example from this Matthew passage, what does it mean to fail forward?*
- *How does the idea of failing forward rather than backward encourage you to take risks?*

Partner - optional (15 minutes)

Reflect
- *In groups of 2 or 3, have women share the risk God is asking them to take, using the reflection questions on p. 132 as a guide.*

Leader Guide

Group (30 minutes)

Reflect

- *Peter found himself back in the boat with Jesus. This wasn't failure, this was the making of a great story.*
- Discuss the first 4 reflection questions on p. 133-134 that follow the statement above.

Leader (10 minutes)

Respond

- Ask women to think about the person whose name they wrote down for the last question - *Whose life might be impacted by the step God is calling you to take?*
- Invite women to find a place to themselves and spend time in prayer for that person whose name they wrote down and the courage to take the step God wants them to take.

Leader Guide

Section 9
Walking Your Friends Towards Healing

Supplies needed:
Bible Study Book
Bible
Journals or blank pieces of paper

Leader (20 minutes)

Welcome!
- *We have spent the past 5 weeks discussing the 5 traits of everyday extraordinaires. So far, which of these traits has stood out to you most and why?*
    - *Everyday extraordinaires listen to Jesus' voice in their storm.*
    - *Everyday extraordinaires step out of the boat and keep stepping out.*
    - *Everyday extraordinaires trust God's limitless power when they are being held back by their own limitations.*
    - *Everyday extraordinaires rise back up and choose not to let fear win.*
    - *Everyday extraordinaires risk, knowing that if they fail, they'll fail forward toward Jesus.*

Group (50 minutes)

Read Matthew 14:34-36.
Reflect
- Discuss the reflection questions on p. 141 about how the disciples may have felt different getting out of the boat than when they first got in.

Leader Guide

Ruminate

- Discuss the table on p. 142, reading the passages and answering the questions.
- *What do you notice about the lengths people took to get to Jesus?*
- *Which of these collisions has the most meaning for you in the place you find yourself today?*

Ruminate

- *What do you think about the statement Willow makes that, "There is just something about Jesus that is so magnetic, so mesmerizing, so life changing, that you cannot help but come and see"?*
- *How have you found this to be true in your own life?*
- Discuss the reflection questions on p. 144-145.

Read aloud Galatians 6:2.

Reflect

- Read aloud the first paragraph on p. 146 that asks us to imagine being there on the shore and discuss the questions that follow.

Individual (10 minutes)

Spend some time journaling about these questions:

- *Who do you want to carry to Jesus?*
- *What do you hope He does for them?*
- *What limits do you put on the lengths you will go to carry them?*

Leader (10 minutes)

Respond

- Invite women to bravely share what they have seen God do in their lives and what they are asking Him to do in someone else's.
- Encourage women to bravely join you in praying aloud for those things.

Section 10
It's Your Turn

Leader Guide

Supplies needed:
Bible Study Book
Bible

Leader (10 minutes)

Welcome!

- Last week we talked about helping carry our friends toward healing. Did anyone have an opportunity to do a little carrying this week?

Group (60 minutes)

Read Matthew 14:22-36.
Reflect

- Since this is the last discussion for this Bible study, encourage all of the women (even the ones who haven't answered much) to be brave and share their answers to the following:
    - *Of the 5 traits of everyday extraordinaires, what trait do you want to grow in and why? And how do you think you can grow in that area?*
    - *What do you need to set down so you can begin believing an extraordinary life is possible?*
    - *When you walked through the reflection questions about your dreams for your life, what came up that surprised you?*
    - *What is holding you back from living out a dream of yours?*
    - *What do you think it looks like for you to begin dreaming again with God in the places you stopped dreaming?*
    - *What do you sense God is calling you to step out of the boat towards?*
    - *What do you think about this statement the study ends on: The invitation awaits... You staying in the boat or you stepping out will determine what story your life will tell. You choose.*

Leader Guide

Leader (20 minutes)

Respond

- Invite women to express how they have collided with Jesus, what they have learned about Him and what they have learned about themselves.
- To end your time together, pray a blessing, over each woman as she hopes to answer Jesus' "go ahead" with her life.

come

collide.

with us

We have more ways you can collide with Jesus at wecollide.net or find us on

Acknowledgements

This project was a collective work of some amazing women getting together and trusting God could use the sum of what we have to do something big. I am so very grateful for these women who poured out their energy, leaned into their giftings, gave of their time, and made great sacrifices to craft this project and get it into the hands of those we believe it will impact. God calls His people the Body, and as I like to say, God gave Collide one hot body! These beautiful women are the hands and feet, the heart and mind, the lungs and mouthpiece being used to bless the world around them and for that, I am truly grateful. There is nothing greater than together handing God what we have and seeing what He can do!

Willow

Willow Weston, Author   *Willow's life is full of crazy, unexpected, broken and beautiful moments that have given way to incredible healing both in her own life and now others. Willow is a sassy, fun, word nerd. She is a spelling bee winner and an eternal 7th grader and is totally fine with it. Willow collided with Jesus and He radically changed her life and now lives to tell everyone else about Him. Willow lives in Bellingham, Washington with her husband of twenty years and her two amazing kiddos. She speaks about God's love at camps, retreats, churches, and other gatherings, in addition to her work as Founder and Director of Collide.*

Michelle Holladay, Content Contributor   *Michelle believes passionately in God's word and loves helping others discover how relevant the Bible is to our everyday lives. Her ideal day would be spent on a warm beach with a good book. One day, she blinked and her two children were grown, but being a mom will always be her favorite job, one she has happily shared with her husband of over 25 years. We are so grateful for Michelle's love of God's word that guided her to help shape, research and edit the writing and content portion of this study.*

Lindsey Kiniry, Graphic Designer   *Lindsey is a rodeo wrangler, a taxi driver, a chaos manager, and a really terrible chef all rolled into one most days. Though she might seem like the life of the party, this secretly shy gal loves to connect with people one-on-one in a quiet space. Lindsey has a husband, 3 kids, 2 cats, a dog and 8 chickens. Her most favorite moments are in creating something and handing Jesus the paint brush. And boy are we glad that Lindsey does because God continues to use her gifts and did so to create the art in this study that so beautifully draws us into Him.*

Anna Kuttel, Project Manager   *Anna seeks to be authentic by entering into others' joy, hurt, and mess. Anna's background is composed of such seemingly paradoxical passions and experiences as anthropology and interior design, real estate and nonprofit, all of which have shaped her into a continually learning-and-growing wife, a mom of two strong and joyful young boys, and a Collide staff extraordinaire. We are ever thankful to Anna for the way she thinks, organizes, administrates and keeps us all in line- this project needed her gifts to make dreams become reality!*